Heritage and Destiny

Heritage and Destiny

BY
JOHN A. MACKAY
President, Princeton Theological Seminary

WIPF & STOCK · Eugene, Oregon

Wipf and Stock Publishers
199 W 8th Ave, Suite 3
Eugene, OR 97401

Heritage and Destiny
The Creative Pattern for Life in Our Time
By Mackay, John A.
Copyright © 1943 by Mackay, John A. All rights reserved.
Literary Estate: John Mackay Metzger
Softcover ISBN-13: 979-8-3852-4240-5
Hardcover ISBN-13: 979-8-3852-4241-2
eBook ISBN-13: 979-8-3852-4242-9
Publication date 1/6/2025
Previously published by The Macmillan Company, 1943

This edition is a scanned facsimile of the original edition published in 1943.

TO THE PRESIDENTS

FACULTY MEMBERS AND STUDENTS

OF TWO GREAT CHRISTIAN COLLEGES

LAFAYETTE AND DAVIDSON

THIS LITTLE BOOK

IS AFFECTIONATELY

DEDICATED

PREFACE

THIS book received its first form as The Lyman Coleman Lectures delivered at Lafayette College. Lectures on the same topic were subsequently given at Davidson College under The Otts Foundation. Between February 1941, and November 1942, the dates when the two series were respectively given, considerable changes took place in the structure of the lectures. This was inevitable, for in the interval two things had happened: the theme had grown in the mind of the lecturer, and the United States had become involved in the Second World War.

But the central thesis of the book has remained the same throughout the struggles of mental composition and the agonizing course of history. That thesis may be stated thus: Inasmuch as a sense of heritage is the chief determinant of destiny, the destiny of man is fulfilled in the sphere of history when God is chosen as his true heritage in personal, cultural, and national life. The subject of human destiny beyond the frontiers of our earthly life, though a most important is yet a different question, and has not been brought within the scope of the present discussion.

For the stimulus to make articulate for college audiences thoughts that were born in the wilds, I am indebted to President William Mather Lewis of Lafayette, and to President John R. Cunningham of Davidson. To these two Christian gentlemen and distinguished educators I wish also to express my gratitude for the encouragement they gave me to give permanent literary form to the spoken word.

I take the opportunity, at the same time, to thank the publishers of the several books mentioned in these pages for their gracious permission to make citations from the same. My thanks are due equally to the authors themselves, some of whose words, together with the inspiration derived from them, I have taken occasion to pass on to others.

JOHN A. MACKAY.

Princeton, New Jersey,
December 31, 1942.

CONTENTS

Chapter One

THE ROAD TO TOMORROW LEADS THROUGH YESTERDAY	1
VOICES OUT OF YESTERDAY	1
THE APOCALYPTIC POWER OF RETROSPECTION	4
BOATMAN PHILOSOPHY	11

Chapter Two

GOD AND ISRAEL	15
THE HERITAGE OF ISRAEL	16
THE SECRET OF RENEWAL	21
THE MAN OF ISRAEL'S DESTINY	26
"ISRAEL ACCORDING TO THE SPIRIT"	30
NEW WATERS OF BABYLON	32

Chapter Three

GOD AND THE INDIVIDUAL	35
CIVILIZATIONS AND SOULS	35
THE QUESTION ABOUT MAN	38
THE CHRISTIAN VIEW OF MAN	45

CONTENTS

MAN'S REMAKING • 48
GOD'S LAYMEN • 52

Chapter Four

GOD AND CULTURE • 57
BROKEN LIGHTS AND EMPTY CISTERNS • 59
THE STRUGGLE WITH FEAR • 64
THE WELL-SPRING OF RENEWAL • 72

Chapter Five

GOD AND THE NATION • 81
THEOCRACY, A QUESTION FOR TODAY • 82
TYPES OF NATIONHOOD • 84
THIS COVENANT NATION • 89
OUR SPIRITUAL HERITAGE • 93
THE HERITAGES OF DON QUIXOTE AND ROBINSON CRUSOE • 98
THE FULFILLMENT OF NATIONAL DESTINY • 102

NOTES • 107

Heritage and Destiny

CHAPTER ONE

THE ROAD TO TOMORROW LEADS
THROUGH YESTERDAY

THERE ARE TIMES in the history of persons and peoples, particularly times of crisis, when a rediscovery of yesterday opens a new pathway to tomorrow, when the awakening of a sense of heritage becomes a potent determinant of destiny. But all depends upon the yesterday to which men go back for a fresh start. Whether the new beginning leads them eventually to a better or worse estate depends upon the heritage they choose out of yesterday as their most coveted possession. For out of the past man may choose God or a "god" as his heritage and the inspiration of his life.

Though these matters had engaged my thought for a good number of years previously, the question of the causal link between heritage and destiny in the life of mankind arose in my mind quite casually, in the course of a visit to California. I shall begin, accordingly, by describing how this particular question came to me, and how it is thrust violently upon us by the realities of the contemporary situation. In subsequent chapters we shall discuss the intimate bearing which the question has upon some of the most crucial problems of personal and corporate life in our time.

VOICES OUT OF YESTERDAY

On a Saturday afternoon in the month of July, 1940, we arrived in our car at the Black Hills of South Dakota. Wind-

2 HERITAGE AND DESTINY

ing up the mountain side through the pine woods we reached a cabin at the foot of the Rushmore Memorial, where we lodged for the week-end. Among the books in our small travelling collection was a volume that had been sent me for review by the Hispanic Section of the Library of Congress. The book, which bore the somewhat unusual title of "Man as Method," was the work of a young Bolivian sociologist, Humberto Palza S.[1]

The theme discussed by Sr. Palza in his book has been a favorite with Latin American writers for some time. Emphasizing the fact that Latin American civilization has been hitherto purely imitative, and that the type of civilization, European in origin and capitalistic in character, which has dominated life in the Southern continent, is clearly entering its twilight phase, the writer raises the question of the future of the Indo-American countries. Being himself a Bolivian, Sr. Palza would like to think that Indo-America included all the members of the Latin American group of nations; but, of course, he has in mind more particularly those countries in which the Indian strain predominates, namely, the lands of the Andean chain from Mexico to Bolivia.

According to this South American writer, a new anthropology needs to be developed which shall consider Indo-American man as a spiritual being, the product of racial and historical factors. If Indo-America, he says, is to fulfill her cultural destiny in the world of tomorrow, she must come to know her true self. In doing so she must discover for her direction the essential principles of thought that spring from the modes and traditions of her own life history and racial background. As the German philosopher Kant discovered the laws by which the human mind as such operates, it is

THE ROAD TO TOMORROW 3

necessary for some anthropological Kant to discover the true laws of the Indo-American spirit. Only by grasping Indo-America's essential heritage from a racial and historical point of view will it be possible to guide her towards the fulfillment of her destiny.

In his own way and from a regional point of view, our author here raised the vast and crucial question of the relationship between heritage and destiny in peoples, cultures and persons. What constitutes the true heritage of a people, a culture, a person? How far is the destiny of these determined by their sense of heritage?

The atmosphere of the gorgeous hills where we sojourned that week-end was propitious for pondering a question of this kind. To my pensive mood the solitude of the rocks and pines and the Sabbath quiet seemed to become vocal with the antiphonal voices of two men, one a German, the other a Spaniard. Both had been obsessed in their life-time with the problem of destiny; both had greatly influenced the Hispanic American mind. There was the stoic voice of Spengler proclaiming that Western culture, being, like every culture, cyclically conditioned and essentially biological in character, would pass automatically away. And there was the Christian voice of Unamuno, apostle of immortality and greatest of modern Spaniards, for whom an individual and a nation find their true self when they come face to face with the Eternal, and discover their true destiny when they allow the Eternal to dominate the springs of their life.

When those voices became silent, the Rushmore Memorial spoke its message. Towering in sculptured grandeur above our cabin stood that greatest of American monuments. Chiselled in the granite mountain side four august faces looked out above the pines, symbolizing four phases of our national heritage. In the countenances of George Washington and Thomas Jefferson, of Abraham Lincoln and Theodore Roosevelt, our heritage of political independence and of democratic freedom, of national unity and of international concern, was engraven. The question could not but arise: How far do these faces enshrine the complete American heritage? And this other: How far do they point the road of national destiny?

On that same evening after night had fallen and we looked forward to resuming our westward course at dawn, another book, the Book, spoke its message in our cabin. We read together: "Whom have I in heaven but thee? And there is none upon earth that I desire beside thee. My flesh and my heart faileth: But God is the strength of my heart and my portion for ever." [2]

"I have said unto the Lord, Thou art my Lord: I have no good beyond thee. . . . Their sorrows shall be multiplied that exchange the Lord for another god. . . . The Lord is the portion of my inheritance and of my cup: Thou maintainest my lot. The lines are fallen unto me in pleasant places; Yea, I have a goodly heritage. . . . Thou wilt shew me the path of life. . . ." [3]

THE APOCALYPTIC POWER OF RETROSPECTION

The reawakened interest in yesterday and its heritage which we witness at present throughout the world is a phase, in a sense the most important phase, of the contemporary interest in the real. In these days diverse forms of realism have taken the place of idealism. A host of people,

THE ROAD TO TOMORROW 5

especially young people, in different parts of the world, have entirely lost faith in ideals, which they have come to regard as deceptive creations of the mind. They have committed themselves instead to what they regard as realities, concrete things that belong to life and history, especially the life and history of their nation, things that they can feel and not simply think about. The quest of our Bolivian for the real heritage of the Indo-American peoples, in order that it might become the basis and starting point for an ideal destiny, is an illustration of something profoundly significant that is taking place in the world. The ideal is now being evolved from the real, and not the real from the ideal, as was the case a generation ago. Let me illustrate my meaning.

The year the First World War came to a close a book was published in England called "The Science of Power." Its author was a well-known sociologist, Benjamin Kidd. Kidd's thesis was that "there is not an existing institution in the world of civilized humanity which cannot be profoundly modified or altered or abolished in a generation." All that was needed was that those interested in accomplishing revolutionary change should succeed in arousing sufficient emotion around the ideal they proposed. The "emotion of the ideal" was his formula; the science of generating this emotion he held to be the true science of power and the key to civilization. In support of his thesis, Kidd instanced two cases: the case of Japan, which in two generations passed from feudalism to a vanguard position among world powers, through commitment to the ideals of political liberalism; and the case of Germany, whose sensibility had been changed in a single generation before the First World War.

If the author of "The Science of Power" were alive today

he would find that in the last two decades his thesis had been both vindicated and refuted. He would discover that, not in a generation, but in a quarter of a generation, in the years, namely, between 1933 and 1939, the German people underwent a much more radical transformation under the influence of emotion than anything that happened to the generation that fought the First World War. On the other hand, he would discover that it was not the "emotion of the ideal," but rather the "emotion of the *real*," that produced this total change.

In the interval since Kidd wrote, a people famed for their devotion to ideas and to the construction of idealistic schemes turned in the abyss of their misery from the ideal to the real. The most real thing they could discover was their racial heritage. The deification of Nordic blood as the ultimately real, its enthronement for the adoration of a despairing people, and the ascription to it and to them of a messianic world mission unleashed the horrors of the Second World War. The leaders of the new Germany repudiated the heritage of culture to which their country had made so rich a contribution. They swept out of their tradition such illustrious Germans as Heine and Goethe, Bach and Luther, and idealized the lusty pagan childhood of the Nordic race. In her abyss of despair and with her future enshrouded in thick darkness, Germany looked back to her most primitive beginnings. The true Germany was identified with an untainted racial inheritance, transmitted through the bloodstream and wedded to a soil as sacred as the soil of Palestine. The determination to cherish and defend this heritage against all comers, and to prove it to be the heritage of the master-race, set the nation on the new path of destiny.

THE ROAD TO TOMORROW

The same is true in the recent history of Japan. It may have been the "emotion of the ideal" that led Japan towards political liberalism in her first modern era, in which, in so brief a time, she recapitulated the progress of centuries. But it was the "emotion of the *real*," symbolized and engendered during the last decade by the enforced devotion at Shinto shrines, which produced the Japan that has proclaimed the new order in Asia and conquered Malaya, the East Indies and Burma. For the leaders of the new Japan the real consists in their imperial house, divine in its origin and pre-Christian in its historical appearance. For them the pathway of the future lies in the passionate fulfillment of the inherent world mission of the people whose supreme heritage is this royal dynasty. And so Japan, becoming dramatically conscious of the ancient biological heritage which she possessed in an unbroken chain of rulers, felt called to the mission of making her Mikado, descended from the Sun Goddess, the creator and ruler of the new order in Asia.

Something similar happened in Russia. In 1917 Russia renounced definitely her imitative role in civilization, together with the ideals of Europe and of Western culture which had inspired her rulers. She renounced the aristocratic Prussian traditions of her ruling class, the Gallic influence that had controlled Russian letters, and the Byzantine version of Christianity that had dominated her religious life. In their stead she chose as the symbols of her true heritage the hammer of the workman and the sickle of the peasant. For workmen and peasants more truly belonged to the Russian soul, the Russian soil, and the Russian past, than Czar or Patriarch. Only those who earned their living by the sweat of their brow or by the fever of their brain were now recognized as part of holy Russia. To this heritage of proletarian workmen and intellectuals Russia linked her destiny.

The Italian cycle in these last years is not very dissimilar. After a period of political liberalism and the threat of a socialist revolution, Italy turned away from the sharp growing pains of democracy and looked back to the days of Rome's glory. Choosing the empire of Augustus as her heritage, she linked her destiny to the dream of its restoration. Mussolini considered it his mission to bring back in greatly enhanced splendor the glory that was Rome. From the moment the Duce chose a heritage for the Italian people in the annals of their past, history became a closed book, with only one possible interpretation, that imposed officially by the Fascist party. Thought must henceforth be focused exclusively upon the improvement of today and the shaping of tomorrow.[4]

It is worth pausing a moment at this point to remind ourselves of a much forgotten fact which has special importance for the Western world. The first great revolutionary movement of modern times, which presaged the new quest of the real in the yesterday of national life, was the Mexican Revolution of 1910. This important movement, so little understood yet so prophetic in its significance, was in its essence the revolt of aboriginal America. It was the precursor of the subsequent revolts of aboriginal Russia, aboriginal Germany, and aboriginal Japan. Mexico, which, in the era of the Dictator, Porfirio Díaz, was committed to the imitation of European, especially French, culture, as her ideal, suddenly repudiated the European, the Hispanic, and the Christian traditions. The key to Mexico's national history since 1910 is a revolutionary process whose deliberate aim has been to

THE ROAD TO TOMORROW 9

slough off the inheritance received from Spain, and to rediscover and express in terms of today the inheritance derived from Aztecs and Mayas. The revolutionary objective was to make this ancient heritage of blood and spirit the basis and starting point of Mexico's cultural destiny. But happily Mexico, the first modern country in which the rediscovery of heritage had revolutionary results for national destiny, has not followed the totalitarian path towards tomorrow.

The significance of these revolutionary political movements, which had their origin in the linking of destiny to some deliberately chosen heritage, might be interpreted thus: The revolutions of modern history, the period dating from the Renaissance and the Reformation, have all been movements that had their origin in the power of ideas. This is true whether we consider the revolutionary movements in England and Scotland in the seventeenth century, the American and French Revolutions of the eighteenth century, the Latin American struggle for independence in the nineteenth century. The power of ideas was never stronger than in the great German idealists before Marx and Nietzsche.

Then three things happened in the secular order that profoundly shook the status of ideas and ideologies. First, Karl Marx interpreted all ideas and theories about human life and the universe as ideologies inspired and conditioned by vested class interests. While, of course, he could not offer any explanation of life or even formulate his own scheme of dialectical materialism without the use of ideas, he insisted, nevertheless, that his scheme of ideas was a transcript of things as they really are in the cosmos. In doing so he made his starting point for revolutionary change in society a concrete social class, to which the future belonged in the cosmic

HERITAGE AND DESTINY

scheme of things. Lenin adopted this class as the heritage and concern of holy Russia and, with the banner of Proletarianism, inspired the Russian Revolution.

Next came Nietzsche's repudiation of reason as a creative and directive force, and his substitution for it of life in all its potency and ardor. No longer was the Rational the Real, as in the days of the great idealists, but the Real was the Irrational, the incalculable, the vital. Nietzsche's exaltation of the frenzied Dionysus was at once a parable and rallying point of a profound change that was taking place in the human spirit as men sought new meaning in life and new power to live. Nietzsche subsequently exulted in Wagner's idealization of primitive Nordic personalities and the pristine Nordic tradition. Yesterday was getting ready for an eruption into today, heritage was preparing to shape destiny.

The First World War, with the abysmal disillusionment that followed the peace treaties, provided an occasion for the coming of the new dynamic realism. The treaties and the Covenant of the League of Nations represented the last stand of ideas, the last redoubt of their application to human affairs as a whole. In the meantime mystic realities, dwelling in the sacred depths of a nation's past, became the dynamic forces that disrupted her present and opened new paths towards her future.

The common element in these tremendous manifestations of power and self-sacrifice which we associate with Russia, Germany, and Japan, has been what we might call the apocalyptic power of retrospection. All these countries have been inspired to forge a new future, not by ideals which lured them on towards tomorrow, but by mystic realities which they glimpsed in the rapture of a retrospective gaze

THE ROAD TO TOMORROW 11

and which have steadily propelled them onwards from behind. Once again in history we have been confronted with the paradox that there are times when strong, adventurous spirits move forward by looking backward.

BOATMAN PHILOSOPHY

What is the answer to the world-shaking, history-determining influence of the retrospective gaze and the deification of a heritage derived from yesterday? The fact that the world is being moved and destiny determined today by passionate realists who discover in some heritage from the past the starting-point for revolutionary change and a new order of life, constitutes a challenge to Christian reflection and action.

To begin with, it is obvious that in times of supreme crisis, when the totally unexpected has happened and life has ceased to make sense, men turn instinctively to simple, elemental things. Truths may then go mad. The desperate instinctive effort to conserve life may lead to tragic waywardness and the creation of monstrous human types, both of which it has done in our time. But this same madness may also point in the direction from which must come the solution of the problem that gave rise to the aberration.

The solution in question is that we must cultivate once again the habit of retrospection. Men must learn to look back if they are to succeed in moving forward. Behind us are the wisdom and experience of the ages. The past is full of landmarks and danger signals which he must study who would advance into tomorrow along the highway of true progress. To look back, and even to retrace our steps for a time, need not be a flight from reality and the hard problems of the present, nor yet an attempt to idealize or divinize the by-gone. In striving to recover a sense of history and tradition we need not become traditionalists and bind ourselves to a changeless yesterday. Still less must we ever succumb to the sin of the Fascists and regard history as so sacred that it should not be discussed. It behooves us rather to realize that too long and too exclusively we have cultivated the forward view. We have been chauffeurs, whose passion has been movement and power and speed. There was no problem so long as we had highways and sign posts and charts. But when the highways to tomorrow became blocked, when forward-pointing fingers became meaningless relics, when charts were useless, when dark clouds settled upon the horizon whither we were bound, and when eruptions began to take place and chasms to open in the fair expanses of civilization which we had never expected to see laid waste—then we became bewildered and directionless.

In such a case what we need is to look back, to cease being high-powered chauffeurs, the slaves of a merely forward view and a false conception of progress, and become boatmen. Why boatmen? Because the boatman moves intelligently forward by looking backward.

Meaning and clarity may be helped if I strike another lyrical note. An experience of early boyhood has become for me, with the passage of the years, a parable and an inspiration. I suppose that when all is said, memories of youth supply much of the stuff out of which philosophies of life are woven.

My summer vacations were usually spent by the shores of a sea loch in Western Scotland. The local fishermen taught me where the best haddock banks lay, and how to find my way thither by observing certain landmarks in the hills behind

THE ROAD TO TOMORROW

the shore. For the banks were not marked by floating buoys by which one could guide one's course towards them. On an early morning I would sit down at the oars and head my boat for the deep water. When, after a time, the roof of the Laird's house became just visible above a clump of trees, and the white foam of a mountain torrent peered over a great boulder of rock, I knew that, at the point where those two lines of vision crossed, lay the bank, and that it was time to ship my oars and drop anchor for the fishing. I had moved forward to my destination, guided by landmarks on the receding shore.

The Christian religion has the answer to the realistic interest in yesterday which has inspired the revolutions of our time. It has the solution to the quest of desperate men who seek in the past a mystic heritage peculiarly their own which they can possess and cherish, and through loyalty to which they may become strong and have the assurance of a significant future. What marks off Christianity from every other religion and life philosophy is the stress it lays upon the retrospective gaze. The word "remember" is the chief word in the Christian religion, as it is the most dynamic word in human speech. The most sacred command in the Bible reads: "This do in remembrance of me."

Truth that is specifically Christian is historical truth, not the timeless, disincarnate truth, in which idealistic philosophies revel. Christian truth has significance for men and wields power over men, because of its relation to history and personality. Yesterday the Eternal entered into the temporal sphere in such a way that it is in and through history, and for the sake of history, that God became manifest. That being so, history possesses timeless significance. Whoever, therefore, would discover everlasting truth about man and the universe must study the distinctive manifestations of the Eternal in history.

God, our Contemporary, becomes known to us in the life of today as we study the record of His self-revelation in the past. He comes to us first in memory, in an act of retrospection, as we scan the Record. Trails appear which bear the footprints of the Almighty; then come places linked to acts of God which changed world history. We meet faces in whom the light of the Eternal shines; we hear voices that convey to us words of everlasting wisdom. Those trails and places, those faces and voices, all point to One in whom God became manifest in the flesh. To meet and submit to God as we find Him in Christ, and, in faith, accept Him as our heritage, our chief good, is to enter upon a new path of destiny. For the God who comes to us out of Yesterday sets our feet upon the path of Tomorrow. For Today and its tasks He is ours in sovereign lordship; we are His in humble service.

All which will become clearer as we explore our theme and seek to establish our thesis, first in the life of Israel, and thereafter in the life of the individual, in the life of culture, and in the life of the nation.

CHAPTER TWO

GOD AND ISRAEL

IN NO PEOPLE known to history did the twin sense of heritage and destiny play so large a part in national life and thought as it did in ancient Israel. Nowhere else in history or literature does God appear as the supreme possession and fulfillment of human life, as both the source and goal of man's existence. In the life story of the Hebrew race, as recorded in the Bible, the dramatic truth is portrayed that the destiny, whether of a people or a person, is determined by the attitude they take up towards God and His purpose.

In these pagan years, when the successors of ancient gods are acclaimed in vast areas of the world, it is natural that the Hebrew race, with its austere monotheistic tradition, should be the butt of virulent attack. It is not surprising that the "messiah" of a "divinely" chosen and self-sufficient master-race of our time should heartily abominate the race which, historically, has claimed to be the "chosen people," the race upon whose racial purity that of Nazi Germany is patterned. Nor is it strange that a neo-pagan like Ezra Pound should regard Jehovah, the God of Israel, as a "Semitic cuckoo's egg laid in the European nest." Like the Japanese invaders of China, Pound prefers the four classics of Confucius to the Hebrew-Christian Scriptures. Thomas Mann, on the other hand, a much greater than Ezra Pound, makes the beginnings of the Hebrew race the theme of his great trilogy,

16   HERITAGE AND DESTINY

"Joseph and His Brethren." Let our retrospective gaze follow that of the exiled German novelist in search of Israel's heritage.

THE HERITAGE OF ISRAEL

The Hebrew people had their home in an insignificant mountain territory in the Near East, situated on the Mediterranean seaboard, and lying athwart the immemorial path of empire. Abraham, their ancestor, was a man from ancient Ur, who, stirred by a deep religious experience, elected voluntary exile from civilization, adopting the life of a nomad sheik. He became a pilgrim and sojourner under the leadership of the God who had called him to a new life and an alien land, promising him and his descendants a world-significant destiny. More immediately, the Hebrew people are children of Jacob, Abraham's grandson, known also as Israel, about whose twelve sons Thomas Mann has written the great book already referred to.

During two thousand odd years this people passed through a series of dramatic experiences: four centuries, mostly of oppression, in Egypt; a life of wandering in the desert of Sinai; imperial glory in the times of David and Solomon; periods of exile to Assyria and Babylon; and finally, total dispersion in 70 A.D., when the Roman Emperor Titus destroyed Jerusalem, their Holy City. Thereafter Judea "dissolved like a pearl in the cup of the universal communion." Today, two millennia after the Jews ceased to exist as a nation, they live scattered throughout the world, millions of them being nomads and captives and exiles, as they recapitulate once again their ancient story. Yet this story continues

GOD AND ISRAEL

to be the most significant in human annals and the most fraught with destiny.

As we study the history of Israel we are gripped by a pervasive, over-mastering sense of the reality of God. The narrative, taken as a whole, aims at conveying the idea that, first under the lowly form of a tribal deity, the one universal God, the "God of the whole earth," manifested Himself in the life of Israel, for a purpose that embraced both Israel and the world. We have here no speculative monotheism. God does not appear in this narrative as the crowning idea of a gifted religious consciousness. The ancient Hebrews, in fact, had no metaphysical gifts like the Greeks and Hindus. They did not speculate about deity; instead of engaging in religious speculation they were constantly forced to decide whether to obey or reject the God who challenged their allegiance. Their consciousness of Him was not the elixir of a highly religious, God-intoxicated people. Nor was their religion an escape from life to a metaphysical sphere beyond personal responsibility. For Israel's God did not drug His people into security; through the lips of His prophets and the dispensations of His providence He goaded them into responsible action, countering their native tendency to be complacent. For them, therefore, true wisdom was not speculative but practical, consisting primarily in the "fear of God," that is to say, in reverence for God.

But God not only pervades, He dominates the history of Israel. He is the hero of the national drama. Not chance as in Herodotus, nor natural causes as in Thucydides, nor the people as in Green, but God, constitutes the basic reality in this history. It is interesting in this connection to compare the

HERITAGE AND DESTINY

Old Testament with Green's "Short History of the English People." In this famous narrative the people stand out as the hero of the book. "Only thus," it has been remarked, "could English history be conceived as a whole. The deeds of kings fall into their proper place, and we hear little of drums and trumpets. Dynasties come and go, battles are won and lost, but the people remain."[1] But of Israelitish history Massilon, the famous French preacher, made the cogent remark: "God alone appears in this divine history. He is, I venture to say, its sole hero. Kings and conquerors appear as the ministers of His will."

When Israel's history is studied from the perspective of the divine Hero and His activity, the category of a "covenant" emerges as the clue to its understanding. The relationship between God and Israel is set forth under the form of a "covenant" between God and His people. Only when this category is employed does the daring magnificence of the Biblical interpretation of Israel's history burst upon us. God "called" Israel, whose life became thereby a vocation. For the "covenant" was not merely a category of religious interpretation, it was a transcript of historical relations.[2]

The Covenant regarded as both category and event, may be interpreted thus: God elects the Hebrew people from among the rest of mankind that He may make them "a peculiar people," "a holy nation." Through great redemptive deeds and chosen personalities He enters into their history, giving them the Law for their guidance. Israel becomes His particular heritage among the nations. God, on His part, becomes Israel's heritage. Perfect mutuality! But as God has so graciously redeemed Israel and given Himself so unreservedly to His people, they must, in like manner, give them-

GOD AND ISRAEL

selves unreservedly to Him and live a life of loyal obedience to His Law. So we read: "The Lord hath taken you, and brought you forth out of the iron furnace, out of Egypt, to be unto him a people of inheritance, as at this day." [3] And again, "For the Lord's portion is his people; Jacob is the lot of his inheritance." [4] Jeremiah, after speaking with great contempt of gods who are no more than idols, says, "The portion of Jacob is not like these; for he is the former of all things; and Israel is the tribe of his inheritance: the Lord of hosts is his name." [5] But God is not merely the heritage of the nation as a whole; He is also the heritage of each pious Hebrew soul. In the Book of Psalms, that chief anthology of religious devotion, we hear, "God is the strength of my heart and my portion for ever." [6] "Thou art my portion, O Lord: I have said that I would keep thy words." [7] Throughout the whole Old Testament we can listen, in fact, to antiphonal voices, a dialogue between God and His people. The divine voice says, "Thou art my people," and the human voice responds, "Thou art my God." In no literature, and in the history of no people, do we find such a case of religious mutuality. Nowhere in the religious history of mankind are the pronouns "I" and "Thou" so transfigured as they are in the history of Israel.

The goal of the Covenant, however, was not racial or national glory, still less the perpetuation of religious exclusiveness. God's election of Israel and His covenant relationship with His people may be regarded as a divine strategy, a pedagogical procedure, the first step in the unfolding of a redemptive purpose that embraced mankind. The election, truly understood, represented neither a limitation of divine sympathy to the elect nation nor a monopoly of divine favor to be enjoyed by Israel alone. Rather was the election, as has been well said, "simply a method of procedure adopted by God in His wisdom, by which He designed to fit the few for blessing the many, one for blessing all." [8]

By adopting this particular approach to the human problem, God linked together religion and history in a totally new way. The core of religion was set forth as responsible personal relations between man and God in daily living. The unique character of the Hebrew view of history has been expressed by Emil Brunner with great clarity and insight. "History," says Brunner, "is that which takes place between the personal God and His people. No other nation, either before or after Israel, ever understood its history in this way. . . . In the national life of Israel the main concern was not with culture, civilization, technique, world-conquest or political power—although these motives certainly often predominated very strongly in actual fact—but with one thing only: the obedience of the nation to its God, and the union of the members of the nation to one another in the community, based upon this relation to God. From the very outset the ethos of Israel is strictly personal and social." [9]

In this covenant relationship between God and Israel, love, knowledge, and obedience were closely linked together. God, unlike the God of Aristotle, was a passionate Lover, who expected passionate love in return. But He was no sentimentalist, nor would He tolerate empty sentimentalism in His people. Their love must not be shown in empty phrases or conventional gestures, but in obedience. And obedience required not merely good will and enthusiasm, but knowledge, that is, insight into God and His will. Inasmuch as Israel knew that her destiny was bound up with loyal obedience to

GOD AND ISRAEL

God's will, sin was a breach of the Covenant, a species of adultery, the worst kind of apostasy.

But the Covenant people, alas, failed to understand and appreciate the true basis and foundation of their life. We hear, therefore, God's complaint, "My people are destroyed for lack of knowledge." [10] ". . . Ephraim is like a silly dove, without understanding," [11] or "without brains," as Dr. Moffatt renders the phrase. Israel's failure in love and practical wisdom led to national apostasy, which was followed, first, by the dispersion and loss of ten tribes among the nations under Assyria, and, later, by Judah's captivity "by the waters of Babylon."

THE SECRET OF RENEWAL

The Babylonian captivity opened a new chapter in the spiritual history of Israel. New notes were struck; new prophetic voices interpreted God, and life, and destiny. In the lonely desolation of their exile, Israel rediscovered the religious significance of the great word "remember." The backward view took on fresh meaning. Listen to the words of the prophet, "Hearken to me, ye that follow after righteousness, ye that seek the Lord: look unto the rock whence ye were hewn, and to the hole of the pit (or quarry) whence ye were digged. Look unto Abraham your father. . . ." [12] "Look away," said he, in effect, to his despondent countrymen who were hanging their harps upon the willows, "look away from these flat, desolate plains, look back to the Judean hills and to the traditions they enshrine of God's dealings with your fathers. Remember His mighty acts and the words of His prophets. Recall, above all else, the great figure and experiences of father Abraham." Let them remember, in a word, their religious tradition, the rock of God's faithfulness and the quarry of their unique religious experience as a race. Too long had they regarded themselves as progressives, cultivating the purely forward look, despising the things that had come down to them from the past, training themselves to imitate the latest innovations of the surrounding nations. Modernity, in its most banal sense, had been their sin. In consequence of that, they had lost their grip on the eternal, and found themselves at the last in Babylonian woe. A fresh start, a new springtime would come to them, said the prophet, along the trail of the retrospective gaze. Let them learn to know whence they were and whose they were.

Another great religious truth that Israel learned in exile might be expressed thus: Life can be renewed, and can acquire renovating power, when God is admitted into its inmost shrine. This lesson the exiles learned from the great visionary, Ezekiel, himself one of their number. Keeping lonely vigil beside a Babylonian river, Ezekiel's prophetic spirit kindled, his imagination caught fire. He saw again, in the full splendor of restoration, the Holy City, which had been destroyed—a new Jerusalem, its Temple towers piercing the morning mists. In a dramatic scene the exiled prophet saw a parable of the basic truth which governed the life and destiny of Israel and still governs the life and destiny of mankind. Here is the truth: Life is true and all is well when God is the heritage of a people or person.

This important truth is enshrined in two symbolical passages: "And the glory of the Lord came into the house by way of the gate whose prospect is toward the east. . . ." [18]

GOD AND ISRAEL

". . . and behold, waters issued out from under the threshold of the house eastward."[14] The glory of the God of Israel broke like a sunrise over the mountains of Moab, the eastern rampart of the Holy Land. Across the Dead Sea flashed the Dawn. Up the steppes of the Judean wilderness the Light streamed, and shot across the Olivet range that looks down upon the Holy City. In concentrated glory it entered the Temple through the portals of the eastern gate, which had been thrown wide open, as if to receive some distinguished visitant.

God's entrance into the Temple was no empty pageant. The holy place where the divine splendor made its abode became a fountain, the source of a life-giving river. By a mystic alchemy, light was transmuted into water, brightness into power. Jerusalem, whose perennial problem has been its lack of water, a lack which always made it vulnerable in times of siege, gave birth to a flowing stream. Through the same eastern portals where the brightness of God had entered, waters gushed forth.

Unfed by confluent streams, the mystic waters from beneath the altar flowed downward with ever-increasing volume through the wilderness, which at their passage was changed into a garden. Laved by the sacred river, the blistered steppes of Judea became a Palestinian California. Fruit-bearing evergreens lined the banks. From the boughs of those trees the dwellers of the wilderness plucked a monthly harvest to satisfy their hunger, and with the leaves they cured their sicknesses.

But the wilderness was not the ultimate goal of the river. Its destination was the Dead Sea, that chief blot upon the face of nature. This was the sea that from time immemorial had turned the melted snows of Hermon, and the blue waters of the Galilean lake, and the rushing Jordan, into a stagnant pool of death. But the moment the waters, born in the sanctuary, flowed into the ancient sea, its age-long reproach was removed. The briny sepulchre soon teemed with fish. Around its barren, solitary shores fishermen plied their craft. The erstwhile tomb of nature throbbed with new life and activity. The sea of death had become a sea of life. No longer did it gluttonously take everything and give nothing in return.

The meaning is plain. Until God had entered the Temple, the latter was no more than a museum of sacred relics and antiquarian symbols. It was cold, empty, and incomplete, for the splendor of God was lacking in its holiest place within the veil. Thus Ezekiel taught the exiles that God's presence at the center of life gives birth to redemptive power. This power is double. It brings life where death reigns. But it does more: it destroys the principle of death, the seat of death itself. By accepting the full lordship of God, Israel would fulfill a redemptive mission, channeling God's redemptive power to moral waste lands, causing them to "blossom like the rose." And beyond that would be the final task of God's redemptive power, the conquest of spiritual death, whose essence is selfish self-centredness, like the Dead Sea. For in things human, self-sufficiency and self-centredness mean death, whether in persons, peoples, or institutions. And for such a living death there is but one cure—a tide of redemptive energy mediated by lives into which the Glory has entered. Thus disconsolate Israel, which had missed the way, received a new view of God and her own mission.

GOD AND ISRAEL

The greatest thing, however, that the Exile did for Israel was to concentrate the thought of the people upon the figure of the Messiah, the coming Deliverer. Their conception of God purified, their native trend towards idolatry and polytheism killed for ever, the Jews became deeply aware of their mission to the world. Israel's world destiny was to be ushered in by the appearance in power of the Messianic King. The Messiah would receive from God "the uttermost isles for His possession." Peace and righteousness would flourish in His time. The earth would then be "full of the knowledge of the Lord as the waters cover the sea." Egypt and Assyria, Israel's ancient enemies, would then be one with her, heirs together of the same promise. Zion would be the great "mother" of the nations. Jerusalem would be the "navel" of the earth, as the Greeks had conceived their Delphi to be.[15] Then would all people come up to Jerusalem to worship the King, the Lord of Hosts.

But Israel did not understand the prophets. The people failed to realize that the Messiah was to be a sufferer, and that, through suffering, He was to conquer and reign. It was part of the tragedy of Judaism during the period from the Restoration to the death of Jesus Christ that the great passage in Isaiah referring to the suffering servant of Jehovah was never applied to the Messiah Himself. Israel failed to keep pace with God and the unfolding implications of the ancient Covenant. The people doggedly regarded the Law of God, the Torah, as their chief heritage. God Himself, who had been their fathers' heritage, became more and more inaccessible. The time came when it was not even permitted to pronounce His august name. The Jews in the meantime linked their destiny to the coming of an earthly conqueror like David, who would deliver them from their enemies. For that reason they utterly failed to recognize the next phase of the self-condescension, the redemptive strategy of God, when He "stooped to conquer."

THE MAN OF ISRAEL'S DESTINY

At length the "Day" came and the "Daystar" appeared. In the triple perspective of Jewish, Christian, and secular history the lifetime of Jesus Christ may be described as the "fullness of time," as "high time," as *Kairos,* the central and most significant point in world history. A man appeared in history who proved to be the Man, history's center because history's Lord.

The amazing thing about Jesus, the Nazarene, who was born during the reign of Caesar Augustus, was His God-consciousness. He was the perfect Israelite, the ideal child of the Covenant, one for whom God, whom He called His Father, was everything, whose meat and drink was to do the Father's will and fulfill His God-given mission. Never had the first possessive adjective been used with such intense meaning in reference to God as when Jesus said, *"My* Father." In the most absolute sense God was His heritage, His life, His all. His destiny was regarded by Him as inseparably linked to loyalty to the will of God. When He talked He did so with authority, speaking "things," and not mere words. When He acted it was with the "loveliness of perfect deeds." In His life, as in that of no other in history, theory and practice, precept and example, word and deed, were one.

But against the Man from Nazareth the Jewish Church and the Roman State combined to terminate His days. Both

GOD AND ISRAEL

feared Him. Caiaphas, the High Priest, represented Judaism's fear for the religious heritage of Israel, if the revolutionary ideas and attitudes of the Galilean were to prevail. For the Nazarene, apart from the fact that He was blasphemously familiar with God, was not respectful, Caiaphas felt, towards the divine Torah and its guardians. Did He not debase, moreover, the character of God, picturing the Deity as interested in social and moral pariahs, in tax-gatherers and prostitutes? So the "priests of a pure monotheism" handed over Jesus of Nazareth to the "soldiers of an international civilization," who crucified Him. The most tragic moment in Israel's history was that in which Pontius Pilate offered to spare the life of Jesus, the "King of the Jews," but was hindered from doing so by priests and people, who shouted in chorus: "Crucify Him—we have no king but Caesar." These were tremendously prophetic words. That day the Jews hailed Caesar as their king. With Caesar they have been dealing from that day to this; and a hard task-master he has proved.

In the meantime the Messiahship of Jesus Christ continues to be the main issue between Jews and Christians. Franz Werfel, one of the greatest of modern Jewish writers, has dramatized this issue in a remarkable play.[16] Saul the Pharisee, now Paul the Christian, returns from his missionary journeys to Jerusalem and seeks out his old beloved teacher, Gamaliel, who welcomes him with great affection. In the religious circles of Judaism, Gamaliel stands for joy against the ascetic gloom represented by Zaddok, whose prayers out-of-doors are so fiery that birds on the wing are burned by them. But there are two things in which Gamaliel, who has studied and been deeply influenced by the teachings of Jesus, dissents from his favorite disciple. Paul has affirmed that love has come, and that the Law has been fulfilled. Gamaliel denies this contention, and insists that love *will* come.

The other issue between the two men centers in the person and identity of Jesus. Paul seats himself, as in the old days, at Gamaliel's feet in the Temple. The day is the Day of Atonement. The pupil yearns for the soul of his teacher. With deep feeling he tells Gamaliel what Christ has meant to him, how his loneliness vanished when he came to know Christ. "Why has Loneliness vanished?" he exclaims. "What is this strong exulting love in me? Whence cometh this knowledge of eternity in the heart, that consumes all fear and decay? A transformation! . . ."

GAMALIEL: (*Rising*) Saul! . . . Thou art in the Temple. . . . We wear shrouds. . . . Think of the atonement which I would make on this Day of Atonement! (*Quickly but firmly*) What has the love of thy Jesus changed? It has changed nothing, as His anger changed nothing. He overthrew the money lenders' tables in the Temple, but on the next day they stood there again. *Not* He, and *not* I, can banish evil, only the Law, that mystery that we may live, the holy Tie which binds mankind.

PAUL: Rabbanu speaketh of a *man!* Oh, the world is swallowed up, both Jews and Gentiles, and only thou art here, thou and He. Gladly would I be anathema from Him, if thou, Israel's hero, now, now, shouldest know Him. A Man! Has ever a man conquered death and decay? Has ever a man risen bodily from the dead? The Light which spoke to me before Damascus, was it a man? Was it a man that delivered me from myself? Can a man grant God's renewing grace? No, Rabbanu, He was not merely a man! He wore Manhood as a garment, as thou and I

GOD AND ISRAEL

wear these shrouds. He, the Messiah, the incarnate Shekinah, God's Son, He was before the world came into being. . . .

GAMALIEL: (*Coming towards Paul, breathing heavily*) Saul! Say that He was a man, for thine own sake and mine!

PAUL: How can I? From man new birth cometh not.

GAMALIEL: From man alone it cometh! For this Temple's sake, say that He was a man.

PAUL: Not in the Temple, but on the Cross was the Blood of the Atonement shed. Now is the whole world the Temple of the great Sacrifice.

GAMALIEL: Saul! Here I still stand before thee. Not yet has the immeasurable calamity taken place! Destroy not my work of peace! The Messiah has not come for the Ever-Coming is He! Thou hast never understood the Torah, bad disciple thou! Only in its star-immersing depth abides the Kingdom of God and our ability to receive it. Where the Torah ruleth not there is wilderness and chaos! Do not force a strange spirit between God and Israel's freedom! For Israel's freedom sake say that He was a man!

PAUL: Rabbanu, by the living God I implore thee. Believe! In this hour, not for anyone's sake can I lie.

The aged Rabbi can endure it no longer. He calls Jesus of Nazareth enemy, and feels it to be his duty to murder Paul with the sacrificial knife, even though they are together in the sacred precincts of the Temple. But the knife drops from his hand. He cries out in anguish, while trumpet blasts rend the air on all sides.

Strange things then occur: For the first time in his saintly life, Gamaliel, engaging in prayer, receives no answer from his loving God. "Answer me now," he says, in an agony, "Who is Jesus of Nazareth? . . . Answer! What should I do? . . . Who is Jesus whom they call Messiah? . . . Has the Messiah come? . . . Have we profaned Thy light? . . ." Presently he adds in bitter sadness, "No answer! For the first time no answer! Empty am I like death!"

Word goes around among the priests that the scapegoat, which had been sent out into the wilderness laden with the sins of the people, is on its way back to the Temple. From the wilderness it is returning alive, instead of having been dashed to pieces over a rocky ledge in the ravine, as the ritual required. The cry goes up, "God has not accepted the sacrifice! It is clear. We have not been reconciled with Him to-day. He sends our sins and blasphemies back to us."

Then the worst of all takes place. Marullas, the Roman, enters the inner court of the Temple announcing the coming of a Roman army. The holy place is defiled by his alien presence. Presently Rabbi Zaddok shouts out in a wild frenzy, "Listen! The catapults rumble! The storm rams bleat! The flames roar! The plough crunches over Zion!" [17]

The imperial anti-Christ had come to Zion. The glory of Israel had departed. The Jews ceased to be a nation. Something worse than exile by the waters of Babylon now began. The imprecation, "His blood be upon us and upon our children," became prophetic of the subsequent history of Israel.

"ISRAEL ACCORDING TO THE SPIRIT"

The destruction of Jerusalem ushered in the era of the Christian Church. According to the New Testament and the faith of Christians, the Church which Jesus founded became the successor of ancient Israel. "Israel after the flesh" gave birth to "Israel after the Spirit." The doctrine of the "remnant," which had played so large a part in the writings of the prophets, took on historical reality in that group of

GOD AND ISRAEL

Jewish men and women who formed the nucleus of the new Christian community in Jerusalem. After the resurrection of Jesus had quickened His disconsolate followers into new life, the Crucifixion, from being the most meaningless event in history, became for them the most meaningful. Both in their experience, and as a result of reflection, the Cross became the manifestation of the reconciling love of God.

On the Jewish festival of Pentecost, God came into the lives of the Jerusalem community with transforming power. They became heirs of the Holy Spirit who took abiding possession of their hearts. For them the ancient covenant of law, which had been symbolized by the observance of ceremonies, was transformed into spiritual inwardness of heart. God became their portion in a new and realistic sense, while they, through faith in Jesus Christ as the Saviour of the world, participated in the redemptive activity of God for mankind. Paul, after his conversion, carried the Gospel of the Cross and the Resurrection throughout the Roman Empire. The new community grew in numbers. As it grew it transcended the traditional barriers that had divided mankind. Gentiles were admitted into the fellowship. The status of women became transformed. Masters and servants who were Christian believers began to treat one another with a new spirit.

When Gamaliel in Werfel's drama had asked in his anguish, "Who is Jesus whom they call Messiah? Has the Messiah come?" and for the first time had received no answer to his prayer, Paul responded fervently, "I have received the answer." Taking Gamaliel's hand and pressing it to his forehead, Paul said, "Yes, I have seen God's answer! I was wafted into dusty streets, in harbours I saw ships come and go; sailors sang. I stood among the throng in a great city, and ever must I go—go—go! For the Christ is a tireless hunter."[18]

The Christ proved indeed to be "a tireless hunter." In His Apostles He traversed land and sea in ceaseless missionary endeavor. What Paul called the "mystery" which had been hid in God, was now unveiled. Jesus Christ was proclaimed as the redemptive center of a new world community. In the universal family of Christian believers, coterminus today with the inhabited globe, we have the contemporary fruit of the ancient election of a single, privileged people. This society is the community of destiny, the organ of God to establish in the world a new order, a Kingdom that shall transcend and outlive the kingdoms of Caesar.

New Waters of Babylon

And the Jews, Israel according to the flesh, God's ancient people? Where are they today? They dwell again by the waters of Babylon, where their fathers once hanged their harps upon the willows and said, "How shall we sing the Lord's song in a strange land?" But this time the Jews are not in exile alone. For Christians as well as Jews our world has become an alien world. It is a world in which Christ as well as Moses, the Gospel as well as the Law, have been rejected by powerful peoples, who persecute alike the Church and the Synagogue!

We have come to a time in history when Christians and Jews realize that what is really at stake in the world is the Hebrew-Christian tradition. Both groups need to look to the "rock whence they were hewn." Christians, on their part, need to put on the weeds of penitence because of the treatment often accorded to Jews in the name of Christ. But hap-

GOD AND ISRAEL

pily Christians and Jews stand together today in mutual sympathy as they have not done for two thousand years. The time has come when both must examine afresh their common heritage, exalting what they have in common, and defining clearly and dispassionately the points wherein they differ. Above all they need to direct a common gaze towards the Nazarene who, for both, in differing senses, has been the Man of destiny.

Judaism has never doubted that it has a missionary function. But until quite recently representative Jews considered that that function could best be fulfilled in calm and dignified silence. To quote the words of a Chief Rabbi, "Judaism has in very truth a missionary vocation to fulfill, in the highest and noblest sense of the term, a propagandism which does not rest on the imperfect agency of human words and human persuasion, but on the silent moral force of truth, truth which must and will prevail. The missionary labors of Judaism must be carried on in calm and dignified silence." [19] But it has rightly been pointed out that this "calm and dignified silence" does not come down in the best tradition of Hebrew prophecy. How different from the passionate voice that proclaimed, "Lift up thy voice with strength, lift it up, be not afraid!"

Other voices, however, within Judaism insist that "the mystery of Israel" must be re-thought and Jesus of Nazareth examined afresh. Some eminent Hebrews boldly proclaim that the tragedy of Israel's history had its source in the rejection of Jesus Christ. That distinguished Jew, John Cournos, recently added his voice to that of Franz Werfel in passionate eulogy of Christ. "It has been one of those preposterous, even ironic, mistakes of history," he wrote in the

Atlantic Monthly some years ago, "that the Jews, having achieved the apex of their peculiar culture in Christ, should then have rejected him. It is their supreme tragedy that, having produced Christ, they should have failed in the final effort to incarnate him in life. . . . The history of the Jews then, during the past nineteen centuries, has indeed been a deflection from their spiritual destiny. . . . Why stop at Hillel when a greater than Hillel came after him? . . . We Jews must come to terms with Christianity. It is the only way out for us." [20]

"Look unto Abraham your father" is the voice that comes to Jew and Christian alike. Recapture Abraham's faith for the world of today by adventuring forth into a new, strange land of the spirit, in response to the call of Abraham's greatest Son. In the measure in which Jews and Christians alike find their chief heritage in Christ, the Mediator to mankind of the power and wisdom of God, in that measure shall the Hebrew-Christian tradition reach fulfillment in "a new heaven and a new earth," and "all the families of the earth shall be blessed."

CHAPTER THREE

GOD AND THE INDIVIDUAL

WITH THE FALL of Jerusalem, and still more decisively with the fall of Rome, the individual human spirit acquired a new significance in history. Standing utterly alone amidst the ruins of antiquity, heirs no longer of a stable heritage from the past, men stood face to face with God and an uncertain future. The day of the individual and the Christ, of man and the Man, had arrived.

CIVILIZATIONS AND SOULS

Towards the end of "The Decline and Fall of the Roman Empire," Edward Gibbon refers to his great work in these words: "I have described the triumph of barbarism and religion." By religion he had chiefly in mind, of course, Christianity. It was Gibbon's view that the Christian religion, by engendering in the souls of men a new subjectivity that kept them absorbed in the things of the spirit, pried them loose from their loyalty to the Empire, its institutions and its affairs, producing thereby the disintegration of the Roman State. While Gibbon failed to take sufficiently into account the basic disintegrating factors that compassed the doom of Rome, it is perfectly true that Christians in the Roman Empire did not consider it their role simply to maintain and perpetuate the splendor of Augustus' dream. Their supreme loyalty was to Jesus Christ and not to Caesar. They knew themselves to be "colonists of heaven," pilgrims and sojourners in search of a "city which hath foundations." The truth is that Jerusalem and Rome, the Commonwealth of Israel and the Empire of Augustus, had both to pass away before the Kingdom of the Saints could arrive and grow. Annas and Caiaphas, Pontius Pilate and the Caesars had to disappear that the new "kings and priests unto God" might take their place. These exulted in their freedom of personal access to the King of Kings and felt themselves to be individually responsible to do His will.

Augustine, in whose lifetime Rome fell, wrote one of the greatest books of all time in order to summon men from the abyss of despair into which they had been plunged by the dissolution of the Empire. But the painter of the new city was the same who in his "Confessions" had said, "Thou didst make us for Thyself and our hearts are restless until they find their rest in Thee." Augustine's deep experience of God, who had become his soul's best portion and his inheritance forever, had taught him the pilgrim way and equipped him for the task of describing God's new order.

In our own time, which is so strikingly similar to that in which Augustine lived, Arnold J. Toynbee, the most distinguished of living historians, has laid stress upon souls as the ultimate goal of both religion and civilization. His study of the rise and fall of civilizations has convinced Toynbee that it is not the function of religion to serve the purposes of civilization, but rather the function of civilization to serve the deeper purposes of religion. Average human nature, he holds, has not greatly changed in the course of the cyclic movement of civilization; what has changed is the degree of opportunity that civilizations offer for the development of

GOD AND THE INDIVIDUAL 37

souls. True progress, therefore, is always progress in soul-making, that is to say, in producing spiritual types of personality. The most effective instrument in creating such types is suffering; for the learning that comes through suffering enables men to "get into closer communion with God and to become less unlike Him during their passage through this world." Civilizations are thus stepping stones to higher forms of spirituality. To quote Professor Toynbee's own words: ". . . If religion is a chariot, it looks as if the wheels on which it mounts towards Heaven may be the periodic downfalls of civilisations on Earth. It looks as if the movement of civilisation may be cyclic and recurrent, while the movement of religion may be on a single continuous upward line. . . . It is this individual spiritual progress in this World for which we pray when we say 'Thy will be done on Earth as it is in Heaven.' " [1]

It might be argued, of course, that Toynbee's view has been influenced by his awareness that the British Empire has reached the most crucial moment in its history. What is really important, however, is his affirmation of the fact that, while the process of soul-making contributes more than anything else to the "improvement of the condition of human social life on Earth," not such improvement, but rather souls, is the ultimate function and test of both civilization and religion. For souls hold the key to every form of human welfare. Thus, to return to where we started, the fall of the Imperial City inaugurated a new epoch in the development of souls, of men who, while feeling that their citizenship was in heaven, were not complacent, self-centred, self-sufficient, or socially irresponsible beings. The spiritual freedom to which they were heirs taught them a new responsibility.

THE QUESTION ABOUT MAN

They were, moreover, not isolated individuals but members of the community, the Church. Man as a mere type had passed away; the Christian man had arrived.

THE QUESTION ABOUT MAN

Who is this individual, this soul, whose spiritual development is served by the cyclic rhythm of civilizations and the straight line march of religion, about whom Jesus said that to gain the whole world would not compensate for its loss? What is man?

Man is still, as he has always been, the great unknown. He is the proper study of mankind today, as he was yesterday, continuing to be the same elusive, mysterious being he ever was. Man in our time is even more strange and disconcerting than formerly. He is more and more of an angel, more and more of a brute, more and more of a voyager between heaven and hell. Today his stocks are down in the world market; he has, in a very real sense, met his fate. We find him in a greater welter than at any previous time in human annals. And many there are who try to "rediscover" him.

The crucial importance of a true conception of man is evident from the fact that civilizations, systems of education, even religions, are based ultimately upon a particular view of man and human nature. We think of such representative types as the saint and the knight of the Middle Ages, the scholar and the gentleman who succeeded them in bourgeois society. Today the chauffeur is our representative type, the man whose characteristic posture is sitting and who, with hands and feet controlling immense power, goes plunging forward at ever increasing speed and with ever greater dis-

GOD AND THE INDIVIDUAL

dain of yesterday. The great importance of having a clearcut conception of human nature is brought home to us by the fact that it was through their respective ideas of man that Nietzsche and Marx exerted the great influence which they did. In fact, the titanic struggle now raging in the world may be regarded as at bottom a conflict between opposing views of man and his status in the universe. The anthropological problem is the crucial problem of our generation.

While our ideas about man and man himself are both in crisis at the present time, there is one thing that inspires hope. Never were men more open-minded and earnest in their approach to human problems; and never was the Bible, that greatest text-book on human nature, more luminous than today. Let us, therefore, in line with this deep concern of our time, turn our thoughts to man. In doing so, let us begin with the question: When is man truly man? What constitutes the essence of man? What is the deepest thing that can be said about human nature? Wherein lies man's heritage? To what is he heir?

Man, it is said, is most truly man when he lives his life as an integral, inseparable part of biological nature. This, in general terms, is the *naturalistic* view. According to a popular version of this view the most perfect man is he who adjusts himself most successfully to his environment, social as well as physical. For what is humanity but a branch on the tree of life? It is the species that matters, not the individual. Individuality, of course, does and must exist but no human being should ever make himself so unique as to stand over against his whole environment. Thus the voice of prophecy dies. Naturalism has no place for it, nor for the hero or the saint. Set to poetry this view proclaims:

> Our strength is as the strength of ten
> Because we are all replaceable men.

This particular view of human nature has caught the imagination and controls the efforts of a great many social scientists. Taking environment for granted they aspire to nothing more than to lead unruly and maladjusted people to adapt themselves to the community of which they form a part. Communities being simply accepted as parts of nature, no qualitative or prophetic judgment can be passed upon them. For this brand of social science a Nazi or a Communist community is basically no different from a democratic community. The problem of adjustment is the same in each case. Obviously, if nature is man's chief heritage and his life continuous with the life of nature, human destiny can never be more than a perpetual adjustment to environment.

For another, a more reflective type of naturalist, the essence of human nature lies in man's erotic tendency. Not a struggle for existence or an effort at social adjustment, but the immensity of desire, constitutes the core of manhood. Desire may take diverse forms: desire for sex experience, as in Freud; or desire for power, as in Adler; or desire in general, *libido,* as in Jung. In every instance man must be allowed to express himself freely. He should be carefully psycho-analyzed in search of repressions, for repressions are the cause of split-personalities. The goal of human nature thus becomes integrated self-expression. The real man is he who desires a thing and succeeds in obtaining it within the

GOD AND THE INDIVIDUAL 41

bounds of propriety and the rights of others. As man can claim no higher heritage than his dissociated self, he can pursue no loftier destiny than its integration. To this consummation all the highest values must be made tributory.

Others hold that man is most truly man when he succeeds in satisfying his basic material wants. This is the *economic* view of human nature, closely associated with the name of Karl Marx. The great symbol of material want is physical hunger, and bread the symbol of its satisfaction. "Give us bread and do with us what you like," were the words which the Grand Inquisitor in Dostoevsky's famous story put into the mouths of the common people. If the Russian novelist had written in America he would, instead of the symbolic word "bread," have used "standard of living." Upon this view all human action and the history of mankind as a whole have been determined by the struggle for bread. What have been called spiritual values are no more than principles formulated by those in power in order to perpetuate their authority over the people who are subject to them. All truth and ideals are thus socially conditioned. They are instruments of servitude rather than gateways to freedom. Man has but one true heritage, and that is "bread," and therefore, but one worthy destiny, which is social security.

According to others, man is most truly man when he is most fully rational, that is, when he lives in accordance with reason. This is the view ordinarily called *humanistic*. Man is regarded as an expression of immanent reason, the principle of universal harmony, in which he participates. "The real is the rational." The basic assumption is that man is naturally good, and that virtue is knowledge. Simply to know that something should be done is itself a guarantee that appropriate action will take place. Education, therefore, is man's greatest need. No extremes of any kind must be tolerated. The great values of truth, beauty and goodness must be pursued in a spirit of sweetness and light. Man being self-sufficient and free, dependent upon no authority but that of reason, it is assumed that there is a natural equilibrium in human nature and that a harmonious balance will inevitably be struck. For rationalism of all sorts is essentially optimistic. The main trend of human life moves, it is thought, towards order and harmony. Thus the ideal man is the man who succeeds in realizing in himself harmoniously all the potency of his nature. He becomes a fully integrated personality, expressing every aspect of human nature and doing justice to all the great values that make up human life. In doing so man proves himself to be self-sufficient, needing no bond to bind him to any other human spirit, in order to fulfill the ideal of selfhood. Nevertheless, men who live under the sway of reason will succeed in giving their corporate relations an equally harmonious expression.

This view of man and human nature constantly recurs in times of prosperity and when society is not being swept by revolutionary change. For that reason it tends inevitably to a detached and contemplative life in him who holds it. It neutralizes that practical effort and that sacrificial lopsidedness which, in days of strain and stress, are particularly imperative. For after all, life's real problem begins when the question is asked: What is a harmonious, well-balanced personality for? If reason, whose symbol is a ball, is to be regarded as man's chief heritage, then no devotion on his part

GOD AND THE INDIVIDUAL

to any cause that shatters this rational harmony can be regarded as his true destiny.

A fourth view is that man is most truly man when he affirms and exercises his will to power. This view is classically associated with the name of Friedrich Nietzsche. The Nietzschean man, or rather, superman, is he who discharges energy, who affirms his independence of nature, bread, and reason. So far as concerns nature, he will not pursue untrammelled self-expression, but will rather exercise austere self-discipline. As regards bread, he will allow no material concern to master him. As for reason, the Socratic, discursive reason, he will scorn its lordship, and will affirm instead the glory of the irrational. "Man," said Nietzsche, "is a being who must be surpassed." He said also, "The earth has a skin and the skin is full of sores. One of those sores is called man."

A superman is a master of men, who has a will to power and affirms life in all its potency. His morality has its exclusive source in his own power of achievement, and he will never submit to the standardized morality of slaves. Might is right. But such a view of man excludes everything that we associate with the name of democracy. It involves rather the permanent relationship of master and slave in a world composed of master-races and slave-races. Between the supermen themselves there would exist no more than Nietzschean "star friendship," a relationship in which those centers of volcanic energy would bow as they passed in the cosmic night, each maintaining due distance from the other and never allowing their orbits to intersect. Thus power is the heritage of true men and by willing power they achieve their destiny.

One has observed in recent times in bourgeois democratic circles the tendency to develop socialized types of supermen. Such people practice a cult of personality. They study the arts whereby personality may become an instrument of power in order that they may be able to control or influence others. This might be called the democratic version of the will to power, a most despicable ideal which permits people to learn the science of social mastery for purely selfish ends. One is even tempted to call this a form of demonism in which men try to introduce themselves into other lives in order to deprive them of their normal powers of self-direction.

These four views of man lack one essential insight into human nature. They fail to recognize that man cannot be understood, that he is not even truly man, save in personal relations. The truth that we are men, not as abstract, isolated individuals, but only in relatedness to others to whom we are bound by the very nature of our existence, is a truth that the views which we have just discussed completely ignore. It is precisely this truth, however, that the totalitarian systems have grasped. Only, they have expressed it in a form which is a most tragic travesty of the true nature of man and of human community. According to the totalitarian scheme of things, a man has no meaning or status save as he is related to a nation, a race, or a class. This relationship forms the core of his human heritage, and he can fulfill his destiny only by subordinating himself utterly to the demands of the collectivity to which he belongs. But man, in so doing, loses his unique selfhood through his complete absorption into a concrete social reality which becomes a

GOD AND THE INDIVIDUAL 45

substitute for God in his life. Not only so, he is pitted inexorably against other nations, or races, or classes, towards which he feels no responsibility whatever. Upon such a basis true humanity in the individual and true community in the world are both rendered impossible.

Christianity has the answer to the totalitarian perversion of this true insight regarding man. It agrees that a self-sufficient individual who has no sense of essential and inescapable relatedness to others is not truly human. It adds, however, that it is in relatedness to God, that man is truly man. Man is man when he takes seriously the fact that he was made in God's image. He fulfills his destiny when he expresses in life the implications of this fact. Let us, therefore, explore the Christian understanding of man.

THE CHRISTIAN VIEW OF MAN

Man is man, according to the Christian interpretation of life, because he was made in the image of his Maker, whose image he continues to bear in a sadly disfigured form. What does this "image of God" in man, this *Imago Dei,* mean? Man, says Emil Brunner with admirable insight, was created by God "in love, by love, and for love." He was made for responsible relations in love. That is to say, he was made for community, for personal relations in love with God and with man. Man, therefore, can never be truly man save in fellowship. It is not some universal reason, or the gift of freedom, or creative capacity, but love that constitutes the core of human nature.

Alas, that for many years now the term love has been degraded. It has become the synonym of a weak sentimentalism which condones everything, from which anger, that "sinew of the soul," and a sense of righteousness, are absent. Or it has connoted a sex emotionalism, a "being in love." But between "being in love," which even at its highest cannot but be possessive, and the love without conditions in which and for which God made man, there is a world of difference. For love by its very nature involves a native sense of responsibility to love others, without consideration of personal advantage. That is to say, man can never be truly man unless and until a sense of community masters him utterly. And this can only happen if God, as distinguished from all craving for fleshly or material satisfaction, from the idealistic desire for self-realization, from a will to power, occupies the high place of selfhood. That great Spaniard, Raymond Lull, said a true word when he remarked, "He who loves not lives not."

It may be objected that this view offers a purely mystical conception of human nature, one that logically involves selfish preoccupation with one relation to God. But to affirm this is to ignore the fact that the love of our fellow men is implicit in the love of God. For as God loves all men we cannot truly love Him unless we are prepared to reflect His love in our relations with others. There is, therefore, no antithesis between the love of God and the love of our neighbor. We cannot love God unless we love our neighbor, and we cannot truly love our neighbor unless we love God.

The essentially social character of the love of God has been admirably pointed out by the great historian already referred to in this chapter. "If Man has been created in the likeness of God," says Toynbee, "and if the true end of Man is to make that likeness ever more and more like God, then Aris-

GOD AND THE INDIVIDUAL 47

totle's saying that 'Man is a social animal' applies to Man's highest potentiality and aim—that of trying to get into ever closer communion with God. Seeking God is itself a social act. . . . The antithesis between trying to save one's own soul by seeking and following God and trying to do one's duty to one's neighbour is therefore wholly false. The two activities are indissoluble. The human soul that is truly seeking to save itself is as fully social a being as the ant-like Spartan or the bee-like Communist. Only, the Christian soul on Earth is a member of a very different society from Sparta or Leviathan. He is a citizen of the Kingdom of God, and therefore his paramount and all-embracing aim is to attain the highest degree of communion with, and likeness to, God Himself; his relations with his fellow men are consequences of, and corollaries to, his relations with God; and his way of loving his neighbour as himself will be to try to help his neighbour to win what he is seeking for himself—that is, to come into closer communion with God and to become more godlike." [2]

When a man responds to the love of God by loving God, and in God loves his fellow men, he becomes in the fullest sense a *person*. Man is man, therefore, when he is truly a person, when he responds to God in love and in love exercises his responsibility towards his fellow men. That is to say, man cannot possibly be man save in social relations. Neither individualism, which is the glorification of the self-centred man, nor collectivism, which forces each individual human being into a pattern, can produce true men. For true men are those who love freely and without conditions, discharging the responsibilities which love brings.

Man's Remaking

But the question arises, How can man as we know him become a man in the sense just outlined, that is, a true person? It is one thing for us, as we well know by experience, to affirm that the true man is the man who loves; it is quite another thing to manifest that love in our own lives. It is necessary to take a very realistic view of human nature. The Christian view of man can be understood only through the light that comes to us from the Bible, which we have already called the great text-book on personality. Especially, we must consider man in relation to Him who, above all others, we must call the Man, the God-Man, Jesus Christ.

Man as we know him has two great capacities: He can transcend nature and make it his servant; he can transcend himself and become transformed into a god. Human sin can be expressed at the level of both these capacities. By his power of transcendence over nature, his own body included, man is enabled to absolutize certain goals in the natural order. He may pursue things, or pleasure, or knowledge, or power, or make it his goal to acquire a personality or to exercise lordship over other personalities. When man does this, banishing God from his consciousness, not recognizing his essential dependence upon Him or his responsibility to Him, he sins. Man can be a sinner, therefore, in the most basic sense, even should he not violate any of the conventionalities prevalent in his age or community. He is a sinner when his acquisitive pursuits are carried on without any reference to God.

Man, however, may not only pursue a host of things acquisitively with a religious passion, he may by a process of

GOD AND THE INDIVIDUAL 49

self-transcendence exalt himself into a god. When this happens he not only makes a god of the objects that he pursues, becoming virtually their slave, living under their control, but he becomes himself a rival of God. This attitude on man's part is the supreme manifestation of sin, for he has succumbed to the chief temptation of his kind, "to become as God." This is precisely the situation that obtains in the present secularized era. It is entirely regnant in totalitarian countries and exists to a very large extent in democratic countries. Men have become as God. There is a religion of man which is not the true religion for man. The religion of Fascism deifies the state; the religion of Democracy deifies man. Both are expressions of man's sinful and perilous rebellion against his Maker, who is the true source of his life and his everlasting heritage. Man, the modern Prodigal, has asked the Father for the portion of the inheritance that pertained to him and has gone away into a far country.

There arises, therefore, the age-long question, the question propounded in that greatest of dramas, the Book of Job, How can man be changed? "What is man that he should be clean?" [3] "How can he be clean that is born of a woman?" [4] Man, the Prodigal, must be made to realize that the world of things, the world that he can possess by exercising his acquisitive capacity, the world of wealth and knowledge, the world of pleasure and power, is purely a dream world. The world of things and sensations and ideas is an unreal world. The real world begins when man encounters a fellow man, when the *I* meets a *Thou* and proceeds to establish personal relations. In this real world, relations must be established to the mutual satisfaction of both parties, that is, in such a way that neither shall by artifice or physical might try to subdue the other to his will. It is, therefore, in the sphere of personal relations that the real human problem begins. It is in this sphere where man has utterly failed and never so much as today. We realize now more than ever that the problem of man's relations to man is such that love alone offers a true solution. But how can true community be achieved in human life? Only when men meet the everlasting Other, the eternal Thou, and become related to Him. Only when man meets God and responds to Him does he become truly man. Only when men meet one another in the love of God does true community become possible.

But how or where can such an encounter take place? Where do we find God? In the person of Jesus Christ, the God-man, as He is set forth in the Bible, which has bequeathed His likeness to today as the chief heritage from yesterday. It is at this point that history becomes fully significant for religion. Here the retrospective gaze becomes the creative gaze, the really forward-looking, long range view. For attention is concentrated upon a redemptive act and a redeeming personality. The starting point of Christianity, as the great Russian thinker, Berdyaev, has remarked, is neither God nor man but the God-man. The presence of Jesus Christ in the historical sphere represents the total and unreserved self-giving of God to man in love. The Cross, which the most enlightened opinion in the Jewish Commonwealth and the Roman Empire could never regard as more than a judicial murder, and which for Grecians, ancient and modern, was a foolish and meaningless gesture, represents, in the thought of the New Testament, God's presence with men in vicarious love, "reconciling the world unto Himself."

In the presence of the Crucified the Christian word "faith"

GOD AND THE INDIVIDUAL 51

takes on new meaning. Faith has been sometimes interpreted in purely intellectual terms, as an assent to doctrines, that is, to true ideas regarding God. Assent of this kind is, of course, a very real part of faith. But faith is not mere assent to doctrines, even to true doctrines; it is basically consent to a Person. It involves the recognition of God's revelation of Himself in Jesus Christ whereby we come to understand ourselves and our human situation and, at the same time, obtain insight into the heart and purpose of God. It involves the total consent of a human personality to God as well as intellectual assent to ideas about Him. We read in the Old Testament that no man can see God and live. When a man meets God in Jesus Christ, who was crucified *by* the world's sin and *for* the world's sin suffered death, faith leads him to identify himself with Christ and with God's purpose in Him as his chief heritage. In doing so he, too, dies, dies to everything in human nature and in history which was responsible for what happened on Golgotha. His old rebellious self cannot look upon the splendor of God's giving Himself to sinful men in love. He learns in experience that the fire of God's love is a consuming flame. And so he dies, committing himself wholly and unreservedly to the Christ who gave Himself for him, and now comes to him and calls him to a new life. He becomes, thereby, God's man, a man who will live by faith in God.

This vital transforming faith will by no means be mere credulity; it will never become a substitute for ethical living; it will express itself in personal participation in God's redemptive work. For "Faith in Jesus Christ is not an interpretation of the world, but it is participation in an event: in something which has happened, which is happening, and which is going to happen. . . . Faith is real communion with the Creator, hence it is not merely a direction towards something future, but it is a fulfilled present. . . ."[5] Faith is, therefore, a new understanding of our nature as man and also a new life. "It means that man, who has been separated, has been re-united, both in knowledge and in love."[6] Thus the man, whose heritage is a reconciling God, becomes a new man, fulfilling his destiny by linking his life to God's great scheme of reconciliation.

God's Laymen

But who is this individual who has come to know himself and God, experiencing in consequence a new life? What does he look like? How does he live? His personal attitude can be expressed in the words of the Prodigal Son, "Make me as one of thy hired servants."[7] His great passion in life is to serve God.

A sense of call, or vocation, if we prefer the term, is the hallmark of the Christian man. He is certain that God has a plan for his life, and he wants to know what that plan is in order to fulfill it. One of the great contributions of the Protestant Reformation to Christianity and civilization was its rediscovery of the common man as one capable of fulfilling a lay vocation as acceptable and significant in the sight of God as the discharge of any ecclesiastical office. The emergence of laymen who, following a personal experience of God, conceived their daily task in business and community life as a call from God, opened a new era in history. The pictorial expression of the new spirit has received immortal form in Rembrandt's great picture, "The Syndics." In the faces of

GOD AND THE INDIVIDUAL 53

that remarkable group of laymen one sees the light of purposeful living under God for the sake of men.

In no single human group was the sense of divine vocation in daily living more potent than among the Puritans who colonized New England. Their extraordinary vocational sense has been finely expressed by the Harvard historian, Samuel Eliot Morison, in "The Puritan Pronaos." Says this distinguished professor: "Fatalism is completely wanting in the New England view of religion or of life. The karma of Buddhism implied a blind, meaningless universe; a poor joke that God played on humanity in one of his idle or sardonic humors. But the Puritans, like the Jews, regarded this earth and humanity as a divine enterprise, the management of which was God's major interest; they were God's people and their God was a living God, always thought of as intensely concerned with the actions and characters of people and nations. Each individual was a necessary item in a significant and divinely ordered cosmos. God has a personal interest in me, and has appointed work for me to do." [8]

Men of that type, about whom we shall have more to say when we deal with culture and the nation, did not make happiness the goal of living. Their consuming concern was to know the will of God and do it. As a result, they found not happiness but blessedness. For blessedness transcends happiness which requires favorable outward circumstances for its fulfillment. Blessedness is a spiritual state, which is entirely independent of circumstances. It comes most strikingly in the midst of suffering, when a man, calmly submissive to the will of God, triumphs over pain and loneliness, and is transformed into a beacon of light and a source of inspiration for a community, a nation, a generation or generations without number.

Jesus Christ did not achieve happiness but He did achieve blessedness. So, too, with many who followed in His steps. One cannot say that Rembrandt and Bach, one the prince of painters, the other the prince of musicians, both of them interpreters of the Protestant religious spirit at its best, ever attained happiness. Rembrandt, at the time he was painting his last great picture, "The Return of the Prodigal," in which the hands of the father upon the stooping shoulders of the boy are such as art had never seen before or duplicated since, was an undischarged bankrupt, who had nothing he could call his own but his clothes and his painting materials.[9] Nevertheless we call Rembrandt blessed because, amid sordid circumstances, he affirmed in that last canvas his deathless faith that the core of reality is the redeeming love of God. Sebastian Bach cannot be said to have achieved happiness. His biographer and disciple, Albert Schweitzer, has said that Bach's own generation had so little interest in conserving his memory that the exact location of his grave is unknown. His skull could not be obtained for the modelling of a bust. "It was only known that he was buried in St. John's church yard." [10] But generations still unborn will call Bach blessed, being transported into the divine presence by the unearthly music of his chorales.

I close with a brief description of one of God's laymen who is nearer our time. Though a person little known, he represents more perfectly than any other in the modern era a layman who conceived his life as a call of God to achieve not happiness but blessedness at the last. Edward Wilson was

GOD AND THE INDIVIDUAL

England's finest painter of birds, an artist, a scientist, and an explorer. Captain Scott chose him to be the doctor and naturalist of the party with which he intended to discover the South Pole. Wilson had accompanied Shackleton on a previous expedition, and some years before Scott's invitation came Shackleton made him a proposal to join the new enterprise. But the naturalist, in the meantime, had undertaken to make a study of the disease which had been devastating the grouse on the Scottish moors. Such was his fine sense of obligation that he turned down the very attractive offer of his friend. But, his obligation completed, the doctor-naturalist embarked for the Antarctic. On the voyage he was the most friendly and most sought-out man aboard. Though he made no great outward show of religion, his companions observed that some time during each day Wilson would ascend to the crow's nest and disappear from view. The study of his diary after he was gone revealed the fact that that lofty eyrie was the sanctuary where he communed with God.

Wilson was one of the little party chosen by Scott to make a dash for the Pole. They reached the Pole in due course only to find that Amundsen had been there before them. They were chagrined to have arrived late but took their disappointment like men, and did not grudge the great Norwegian his achievement and his fame. On the way back, owing to a miscalculation for which they were not responsible, the members of the party were beaten by the Great Barrier and knew that their end had come. Oates, out of consideration for his comrades, walked out into a blizzard. The only men left were Scott and Wilson. They lay down together to die. In a letter to his wife, Edward Wilson wrote these last words in the hope that the message would reach her after he was gone:

"Don't be unhappy—all is for the best. We are playing a good part in a great scheme arranged by God himself, and all is well. . . .

"All is for the best to those that love God, and oh, my Ory, we have both loved Him with all our lives. All is well. . . .

"Dad's little compass and Mother's little comb and looking-glass are in my pocket. Your little testament and prayer book will be in my hand or in my breast pocket when the end comes. All is well." [11]

Scott, who lingered on in life a little longer, glanced at his friend and wrote in his own diary: "His eyes have a comfortable blue look of hope and his mind is peaceful with the satisfaction of his faith in regarding himself as part of the great scheme of the Almighty. . . ." [12] All was well.

Yes; it is the consciousness of being "part of the great scheme of the Almighty" that helps one calmly to triumph over circumstances and to achieve something infinitely greater than happiness. This Edward Wilson achieved. His life mission, with the manifold obligations to which he was so sensitive, had been accomplished. His faithful friend and leader lay beside him. With the tenderness of His Saviour upon the Cross he remembered his father and mother and wife and the precious little things that were the gifts of each. And, with "a comfortable blue look of hope in his eyes," he passed away. A man of God, a truly royal person! Those who read Wilson's life cannot but exclaim, "Behold, a man!" His memory is now part of the spiritual heritage of England.

To the ultimate inspiration of individual souls both culture and national life owe their chief nobility and their principal source of renewal.

CHAPTER FOUR

GOD AND CULTURE

IT IS ONE of the ironies of history that an intellectual period which gloried in its scientific approach to every problem should have left one thing, the most important of all, without criticism or scrutiny. The era, called by Sorokin the era of sensate culture, which refused to take seriously anything that lay beyond the power of the senses to perceive or measure, failed utterly to examine its own cultural presuppositions. The same cultural eye, which pried so mercilessly into all things in earth and heaven, took naïvely for granted its own powers and goodness, although it was actually suffering from a very grave disease. In the last two decades, however, the situation has changed. A critique of culture has formed the theme of a variety of incisive studies in Europe and America.

As a result of these studies the awareness has steadily grown that we have come to the end of a cultural era. A point has been reached in the history of Western civilization when sensate culture appears to be exhausted, with nothing more to give. A "Day of the Lord" has struck it; a new *"Dies irae, dies illa"* has arrived. We are living at this moment in one of the transition times in human history, a time between the times. Our era bears all the marks of judgment, all the agony and scars of the typical transition period. Ours is a world divided largely between ghosts and crusaders: ghosts who stalk abroad moaning or in silence and find no haven of rest, crusaders with martial gait who fill the air with noisy slogans.

In this twilight time certain things have become clear, which might be stated thus: Religion, as Spengler pointed out, has been the soul of every great culture. Christianity has undoubtedly been the most potent and uplifting influence in the culture of the West. Many systems of thought and life that have no place for Christianity are themselves forms of "secularized Christianity." It is equally and tragically true that in the period immediately preceding the Second World War there was no such thing in the secular realm as a culture worthy of the name. To a very large extent Western man, amid all the devices and gadgets of civilization, has been living in a cultureless world. This fact was, and continues to be, a large part of our modern predicament.

But before we discuss our cultural situation it is important to ask what we mean by culture, and what the difference is between culture and civilization. Sometimes these two terms are used loosely and even synonymously. There is, however, a clear, if conventional, distinction between them. Civilization is the body of which culture is the soul. Culture represents spirit; civilization represents organization. Civilization expresses the means by which men live; culture the ends for which they live. A culture, therefore, is made up of the ideas and principles, the attitudes, the spirit and the ethos, of an era.

Some simple examples will help us to get this distinction clear. Take a hospital. Its significance for civilization is indicated by such things as the building, the equipment, and the technical skill of doctors and nurses. Its cultural significance is expressed by the atmosphere of the place, and by the

GOD AND CULTURE

degree of rich, self-sacrificing humanity shown by the members of the staff. It is thus conceivable that an ambulating Red Cross wagon, with a Florence Nightingale or a Wilfred Grenfell in charge, might express more genuine medical culture than the best equipped hospital in London or Manhattan. Or consider an organ, such an instrument as might be found in a great modern cathedral, with every technical improvement in the organ builder's art, suggesting thereby advanced civilization. Yet an old organ, with few technical contrivances, but with a Bach or Beethoven at the keyboard, would represent a much higher degree of musical culture. Without true culture civilization is a shell, an empty pageant, a soulless machine, a garish sepulchre of souls. Culture, when it is true, is spirit and light. But if culture be spiritless and savorless, alas for civilization. Our task in this chapter is to survey our contemporary cultural situation and consider its cure.

BROKEN LIGHTS AND EMPTY CISTERNS

The cultural era which began with the Renaissance and is now in its twilight, has been characterized by a glorification of man, of human nature and human capacity. Self-sufficient, autonomous man was regarded as a perennial fountain of life, a being endowed with capacity to penetrate to the uttermost secrets of the universe. At different times in this period, human thought, human emotions and human energy were successively transfigured. Rationalism, romanticism, vitalism followed one another—until the First World War placed a great question mark after Man. The intervening years between the two wars have changed that question mark into an epitaph. Self-sufficient man has failed. A homocentric culture has ended not only in error but in horror. When we examine our cultural situation today in those countries where bourgeois civilization still continues, and very especially in the United States, we discover two main characteristics. One of these is negative in character, the other positive. The negative characteristic is a sense of emptiness; the positive, the presence of fear. Something has passed away, and something that is most unwelcome has taken up its abode among us.

The pervasive *sense of emptiness* that marks our culture takes many forms. One of these, probably the chief, is an absence of meaning. Meaninglessness manifests itself in an immense variety of ways and in a great diversity of places. Contemporary man has acquired a sense of the abyss. A multitude of sensitive spirits, especially among the poets, have learned the meaning of perdition. They have felt themselves to be submerged in a blind vortex.

> It is the moment of the whirlpool, moment
> Of the abyss where all things stream.[1]

In some circles this sense of the abyss has been deliberately cultivated. Men, though afraid of the abyss, have been lured by it, exemplifying that strange fascination which so impressed the mind of Kierkegaard. Jung has described in the following terms the pathological situation involved. Man today, says he, "has approached the zone of world-destroying and world-creating fire, dominated by the lust of self-demolition."[2] Very striking also are the words of Timbaud, "I accustomed myself to the states of pure hallucination. . . . I reached the point of seeing something sacred in my mental disorders."[3]

GOD AND CULTURE

A host of others have been gripped by a sensation of futility and frustration. Many who do not allow themselves to pine away in morbid introspection and do not take drugs in order to sense the abyss or to escape from it, find life to be a very drab and routinary affair. While continuing to discharge their assigned tasks with faithfulness, they dare not stop to think, for they dread the possible consequences of thought. They live like tight-rope walkers for whom reflection or any attitude but the purely forward gaze would spell disaster and a certain drop into the abyss.

The mists that rise from the abyss blur all moral and other distinctions. After all, what do distinctions matter?

> All's one in the end, republic, dictator,
> We're the lowest common denominator.[4]

More than one critic has remarked that in the modernistic art of our time the clear outlines of the human figure disappear and man fades into physical or animal nature. "Demoralization, dehumanization, brutalization" are words used by the sociologist, Sorokin, to describe what has taken place in the pictorial arts that belong to sensate culture.

Meaninglessness expresses itself likewise in the absence of unity and harmony in modern life and thought. In a sonnet by Geoffrey Scott the anvil takes the place of the lyre as the symbol of poetic inspiration and expression. The sonnet is so striking and so true to a current mood that I quote it in full:

> Now come within, and hearken to my ringing:
> I am the Anvil: on my steely bed
> True dreams are gendered; I have other singing
> Than lyric air in lilted number led.
> My deeds are hopes split on the glitterless dark,

> My music is an iron starry shout,
> My suns are born to briefness like a spark:
> So was man's measure wrought and beaten out.
> Loud in my cave with grinding echoes rife,
> Lean, disaccording, counter-crossed and jarred,
> I mint the carol of created life,
> Chiming amiss with every cadence marred.
> If then, than these, more grateful tunes you crave,
> Choose to be deaf: your music's in the grave.[5]

The smithy is here regarded by the poet as the true pattern of life. Deeds that are "hopes split on the glitterless dark," that are "suns born to briefness like a spark," are an awesome picture of the meaningless welter of light and sound. Life has no central, enduring sun to give it meaning. Personality is dissolved in a tumultuous succession of words, impulses, desires, that can never achieve harmony or meaning.

> All truth alters
> And the lights of earth are out.

This lack of unity is reflected in education. There is no longer any over-arching, luminous idea that gives unity and meaning to the educational process and binds together the several departments in a great university. Specialization has been carried to such a pitch that the experts, the men who "know more and more of less and less," no longer understand each other. To bring this cultural anarchy to an end President Hutchins of Chicago has proposed that university education be informed by some metaphysical concept. A similar concern has inspired the group of scholars who have sponsored for three successive years the "Conference on Science, Philosophy and Religion." The feeling has become articulate that

GOD AND CULTURE 63

it is absolutely necessary in the interests of a unified culture that scholars should be willing to listen to and understand each other. As things stand at present, life is compartmentalized into vacuity. Art is for art's sake; business is business; the scientist is jealous for the honor of his specialty; the philosopher is disdainful of the common herd. In the mean time all sorts of panaceas are offered for reform. "American education," one has said, "is like a man who continuously builds himself new homes and never lives in one. He perishes, running here and there with his stones and his new blueprints."[6]

The source of all our trouble whereby our culture has become so meaningless and arid has been well described by a man who himself began in the wasteland, but succeeded in passing through the desert to a new Land of Promise without being swept into the abyss.

> We set ourselves to grow in the wrong earth
> And now we have no roots.[7]

What is worse, an academic degree as such, without any particular reference to its kind or quality, has become a fetish. "Send me a Ph.D.," said a college president to the dean of a leading graduate school. When asked in what department he wanted a Doctor of Philosophy, the reply was, "Oh, that does not matter. All I want is a Ph.D."[8]

In a situation so meaningless as this what is obviously needed is a transcendent frame of reference, a great luminous idea, a central sun of some kind that would light up our cultural scene. An authoritative voice must also sound if we are to understand ourselves and our situation and discover a path through the enveloping gloom. Otherwise there shall be fulfilled in our time the tremendous words of the Hebrew prophet: "Behold, all ye that kindle a fire, that gird yourselves around with fire-brands; walk ye in the flame of your fire, and in the brands that ye have kindled. This shall ye have of my hand; ye shall lie down to sorrow." [9] For no one can guide his life by the brands of his own interests or specialized knowledge. If he tries to do so he cannot escape a headlong fall into the abyss.

The Struggle with Fear

The second characteristic of our contemporary cultural situation is *the presence of fear*. There is a pervasive fear of life itself. It has been truly remarked that in the ghost stories of the Victorian era the haunted houses were always situated in the suburbs, but today the city itself is haunted. In days past men and women revelled in solitude. Searching for solace from the hard realities of life, they sought refuge in their own spirits or in contact with wild nature. But today the inmost shrine of personality has, in very many instances, been itself converted into a chamber of horrors. Many dare not look within them and many more flee from their own company. T. S. Elliott in "The Wasteland" thus quotes the sibyl, "What is your desire?" "My desire is to die." Hence the great vogue of suicide.

There is a rooted fear of discomfort and suffering. Ours has been well called a sitting civilization. For, although we move faster than human beings have done at any previous time in history, we do so almost always in a sitting posture. A recent writer quotes the advertisement of a telephone company, "Reach for the phone before you reach for your hat." [10] It has also been most truly remarked that "comfort is to the bourgeois world what heroism was to the Renaissance and

GOD AND CULTURE 65

sanctity to medieval Christianity—the ultimate value, the ultimate motive for all action."[11]

How deeply we hate suffering and the symbols and trappings of sorrow in these United States! The perfect symbol of this attitude is that great "Memorial Park" in Los Angeles, called "Forest Lawn." Every emblem of gloom has been assiduously excluded from its precincts. To grace this most marvelous of graveyards, a Christ who smiles has been sought everywhere, but still in vain. Despite the entrancing beauty of Forest Lawn, the question insistently arises whether it is a Christian cemetery or not. For the genius of Christian culture is not to banish from sight the symbols of tragic reality, but to look them squarely in the eye and exultantly triumph over them. All that is greatest in human culture has been born of pain. How true are the lines:

> When the heart is saddest
> The harp's tense strings are gladdest.

And what is true in music is true in all the arts.

Forest Lawn, however, reflects a very decided spiritual trend in the United States. Spanish and Latin American friends have frequently remarked to the writer how strange it appeared to them that portrayals of Christ's sufferings have no place in the vast majority of American Protestant Churches where religious art is used. Upon stained glass windows one will find scenes from the Nativity and from the life of Christ up to and including the praying Figure in Gethsemane. Then the Saviour disappears from view until He appears all radiant on the Resurrection morning. In the Hispanic world the characteristic figure of Christ is the Crucified, who either hangs upon the Cross, or has just been taken down, all gory, by loving hands. Spanish art knows neither the Jesus of Galilee nor the Christ of the Resurrection. If Spanish religion has been essentially a cult of death, Protestant religion in the United States has tended increasingly to become a cult of life on the Grecian model, from which the Cross and everything associated with it have been banned. Pain has come to be regarded as intrinsically an evil. Deep down in the American view of life there is a decided distaste for the symbols of suffering whether in a religious or secular setting. And now that we must suffer discomfort and anguish upon an unprecedented scale, we are singularly unprepared in our habits and ways of thought for both.

In academic circles especially there has existed recently a very decided dread of commitment to a great idea or a great cause that would involve consequent action. Teachers have liked to live in the detachment of Olympus, contemplating life, each one from his balcony, without descending to the road to mingle with pilgrims and wayfarers, or stepping into the arena where battles are fought and won. Unamuno used to accuse the intellectuals of his country of treating ideas as lewd people treat women, using them only as paramours for a night. Take a great idea, he used to say, make it your wedded wife and raise a family. But too often thinkers balk at making an idea bone of their bone, flesh of their flesh and the mother of children.

Shortly after the last World War the French writer Julien Benda wrote a book entitled "La Trahison des Clercs," "The Treason of the Intellectuals," in which he accused the intelligentsia of France of refraining from giving any active leadership to the nation. We know what subsequently happened in the life of the French Republic. And now in a bril-

GOD AND CULTURE

liant little book, "The Irresponsibles," that great American poet, the present Librarian of Congress, Archibald MacLeish, describes the detachment from life of our scholars and artists. We miss, says MacLeish in effect, the old time man of letters who was the glory of our English speaking world, the man who was both a scholar and an artist, and who used his learning and his pen to promote some great idea or great cause. But the scholar and the artist of that type are, with some few glorious exceptions, sadly lacking. The scholar is interested in content; the artist is interested in form. But rarely are scholarship and artistry, truth and beauty, combined in a great passion for righteousness. We may well learn the lessons of other countries where scholars and artists essayed to live a life of similar detachment. The time came when, through their abdication of all responsibility for public affairs, they were no longer free to think or express themselves as they would.

Our institutions of higher learning must share a good part of the blame for the detachment of the scholar and artist from real life. Today, owing to the national emergency created by the war, great institutions have become harnessed to the practical necessity of equipping the country for armed strife. The criterion of national need has become regnant in every academic department. It is a question whether universities ought not to recognize what universities in the Middle Ages recognized, that it is their perennial function to serve a cause greater than the cause of abstract truth. President Lowell of Harvard once defined a university as: "A society or guild of scholars, associated together for preserving, imparting, increasing and enjoying knowledge." Dr. Abraham Flexner, the distinguished founder of that most remarkable institution, "The Institute for Advanced Study," has thus crystallized his ideals for the new home of learning, now one of the glories of Princeton: "It should be a haven where scholars and scientists may regard the world and its phenomena as their laboratory, without being carried off in the maelstrom of the immediate."

The question, however, may legitimately be raised whether either of these conceptions of an institution of higher learning is fully adequate for the necessities of a world such as ours, even in halcyon days of peace. Even a university professor must have a higher aim than that of "preserving, imparting, increasing and enjoying knowledge." For not knowledge, but God is the true absolute, even for the scholar. When God is known, scholarship becomes transfigured in such a way that knowledge and life are passionately linked together in a great concern that truth shall advance the cause of goodness. Even for scholars and scientists who would live a true life and serve their time, the world and its phenomena must be much more than a laboratory. They must be also an arena for action. And such action, so far from destroying the zest and capacity for scholarship, will transfigure the personality of the man and enhance the capacity of the scholar.

Perhaps, after all, it is we professors who are the chief cultural problem. Kierkegaard, who said so many pithy things, once remarked: "Take away paradox from the thinker and you have the professor." At the first meeting of the "Conference on Science, Philosophy and Religion," Professor Adler of the University of Chicago read a paper entitled "God and the Professors" in which he blisteringly indicted the professorial mind. His paper subsequently raised a storm on the campus of Chicago University. Adler gave expression in that

GOD AND CULTURE

paper to some things which those of us who are professors in institutions of higher learning cannot but ponder and lay to heart. Says this professor: "Instead of a conference about science, philosophy and religion in relation to democracy, what is needed is a conference about the professors of science, philosophy and religion, especially American professors whose intellectual attitudes express a false conception of democracy. The defects of modern culture are the defects of the intellectual leaders, its teachers and servants. The disorder of modern culture is a disorder in their minds . . . I repeat my charge. The professors, by and large, are positivists. And, furthermore, I say that the most serious threat to Democracy is the positivism of the professors, which dominates every aspect of modern education and is the central conception of modern culture. Democracy has much more to fear from the mentality of its teachers than from the nihilism of Hitler. . . . If I dared to raise my voice as did the prophets in ancient Israel, I would ask whether the tyrants of today are not like the Babylonian and Assyrian kings—instruments of Divine justice, chastening a people who had departed from the way of truth. . . . So, perhaps, the Hitlers in the world today are preparing the agony through which our culture shall be reborn. . . . It is probably not from Hitler, but from the professors, that we shall ultimately be saved." [12]

Still another fear is the fear of emotion. In both academic and ecclesiastical circles in these last years we have suffered emotional starvation. Dry facts and cold reason have been exalted far beyond their importance. It has been forgotten, as John MacMurray has pointed out, that emotion is as much a part of rationality as the discursive reason.

> Has only reason been baptized,
> Are feelings only heathen?

One would think that they were, so far as classroom and sanctuary have been concerned in these last times. In the nineties of last century a group of Oxford students who had passed through a deep religious experience, young men outstanding in their intellectual attainments and who afterwards achieved distinction in life, swung down the High Street one evening in front of the dwelling of Walter Pater, that perfect Grecian in style and idea. As they passed the window of the author of "Marius the Epicurean," they sang a stanza, which, though poetically pure doggerel, conveys a challenge to many a center of culture:

> It's better to shout than to doubt,
> It's better to rise than to fall,
> It's better to let the glory out
> Than to have no glory at all.

In these years many teachers and clergymen have not known what to do with young enthusiasts. Young men and women bursting with spiritual concern have received scant encouragement from mentors or pastors. They have been considered a peril, most dangerous fanatics. Religious leaders in university campuses and in churches have been scared white many a time by emotional outbursts on the part of youth. Youth have been ready to give themselves to a great cause, and many religious leaders have either not been able or have been unwilling to show them the way. They have tried instead to tone down the spirit and temper the ardor of young men and women, without either understanding the

GOD AND CULTURE

grounds of their enthusiasm or providing an outlet for their zeal. Their whole policy has been directed towards keeping them sedate and "normal." No wonder that so many young enthusiasts have found their way into the ranks of Communism and others into the fellowship of the cults and sects. What is religious leadership prepared to offer as a substitute for the revolutionary fervor of young radicals like those described in these lines of an American poet?

> Our songs had hair and blood on them.
> We had something they didn't have:
>   our love for these States
>   was real and deep. . . .
> Let them burn us, hang us, shoot us,
>   Joe Hill,
> For at the last we had what it takes
>   to make songs with.[18]

Songs "with hair and blood on them"! How do we churchmen propose to deal with the problem presented by those millions who today can find no inspiration for their religious life in the organized churches of this country, and have had to seek religious satisfaction in the fellowship of the sects and the cults? To make worship more beautiful, stately, and reverent will not solve the problem. What is needed is heat, genuine religious heat. We must both learn and live the meaning of the words, "Our God is a consuming fire." Nothing great can be accomplished save through heat, through the influence of a great and pure emotion. "No heart is pure that is not passionate; no virtue is safe that is not enthusiastic." At Pentecost long ago the Spirit came down like "Tongues of Fire." "Maintain," said Paul, "the spiritual glow."

And then there is the deadly fear of tomorrow. In these days of war this fear has been greatly increased. Such is the tyranny of the next day that we cannot calmly and decisively fulfill the tasks of the day that is passing. How easy it is to take a flight in thought into tomorrow in order to escape the unpleasantness and responsibilities of today! How easy it is to think through the kind of world we would like to have tomorrow and fail to act in an appropriate way in the world we do have today! But without such action now a worthy tomorrow will never come. If only we could feel that we were a part of God's everlasting day and fulfill, under His leadership, the tasks of the moment, we should be disposed to leave some of tomorrow's concerns with Him. In front of the actor, blinded by the footlights, there is the deepest darkness, the blackest night. But that pitchy darkness is the condition of his success upon the stage. If he could see before him, his power of concentration upon his immediate role would vanish. "Cram today with eternity," said Kierkegaard, "and not with the next day." The only cure for the fear of tomorrow is a realization of the fact that the eternal God reigns and guides today. Our times are in His hand. If, like the lilies and the birds, we do what belongs to today, God will make that the best preparation for tomorrow.

The Well-Spring of Renewal

There is but one answer to our cultural situation. God. Now, as ever, His coming into life gives birth to a river of destiny. To the voices that speak "out of empty cisterns and exhausted wells," the answer is, "With Thee is the fountain of life." To those who are willing to listen, the voice says, "Prepare to meet thy God." "Throw open the eastern portals."

GOD AND CULTURE

The encounter between the human spirit and the divine is the source of renewal. For there is nothing more real than the meeting of spirits. Let us remember, in our cultural wilderness, the splendor that entered and filled the empty Temple, the water that gushed forth from a "desolate source." The cure for emptiness is the incoming of God into life. The cure for fear is to be swept along in the mighty current of God's redemptive purpose for mankind.

This is what Sorokin would call the reawakening of interest in spiritual, supernatural reality, in what he terms the "ideational." It is what St. Augustine meant by *adhaerere Deo,* "to stick to God." This would mean a return to the true fountain and source of our lives, in search of fullness of meaning, in search of a thrill to banish fear. The Nazis and Japanese returned to their origin in a purely biological sense. We must return to ours in a spiritual sense. That origin is God, the fountain-head of meaning and of life. Let it not be said that by following such a course we represent "the reflex of the aged adult who reverts back to his childhood." No, this is rather the return of the vigorous, puissant boy to the paternal home, a prodigal indeed, but a welcome guest.

The perennial need of human culture is double: the need of knowledge and the need of power, the need of light and the need of strength, the need of guidance and the need of achievement, the need of truth and the need of grace. Both these needs are supplied in a unique way in the Christian religion, in the self-revelation of God in Jesus Christ who is described as being "full of grace and truth." [14] The answer, therefore, to our cultural sickness is two-fold: first, the restoration of meaning; second, the experience of grace. Let me deal briefly with both in turn.

Meaning must be restored to our existence. The first step in the restoration of meaning is the illumination of our condition. We need light to understand ourselves and the situation in which we are found. The only light that is adequate to interpret what we are and where we are is the light of God. "In Thy light," said the Hebrew Psalmist, "we shall see light."[15] This light comes to us in our Christian heritage. It is mediated to us through the Bible. In the luminous deeds, words, and personalities contained in the Book, especially in the face of the "Word become flesh," we come to know and understand the meaning of life.

For two centuries after the death of Johann Sebastian Bach, the meaning of his chorales remained obscure and enigmatic to the students of his music. The solution was not found until Albert Schweitzer discovered that the chorales must be interpreted in terms of the Biblical text which had inspired their composition. Schweitzer's old teacher of music in Paris wrote a preface to his pupil's book on the life and music of Bach. How significant are his words! "One day in 1899, when we were going through the chorale preludes, I confessed to him that a good deal in these compositions were enigmatic to me. . . . Why these sometimes almost excessively abrupt antitheses of feeling? Why does he add contrapuntal motives to a chorale melody that have often no relation to the mood of the melody? Why all these incomprehensible things in the plan and the working-out of these fantasies? The more I study them the less I understand them.

" 'Naturally,' said my pupil, 'many things in the chorales must seem obscure to you, for the reason that they are only explicable by the texts pertaining to them.'

"I showed him the movements that puzzled me the most;

GOD AND CULTURE

he translated the poems into French for me from memory. The mysteries were all solved. During the next few afternoons we played through the whole of the chorale preludes. While Schweitzer—for he was the pupil—explained them to me one after the other, I made the acquaintance of a Bach of whose existence I had previously had only the dimmest suspicion." [16]

"They are only explicable by the texts pertaining to them." Contemporary culture needs to be confronted with the Christian revelation. The Bible, containing as it does the record of the self-disclosure of God and His will for human life, is the only Text that can explain to us our thoughts and our aspirations, our aberrations and our tragedies. When this Text is studied the enigma of life's strange, meaningless music becomes plain, and the nature of our predicament is made clear to us. Modern culture went astray by giving to man the place that belongs to God. Let us heed, accordingly, the prophetic words, "Cease from man"! [17] Elsewhere we read: "They have forsaken me, the fountain of living waters, and hewed them out cisterns, broken cisterns, that can hold no water." [18] This is exactly what we have done. Therefore our cisterns are empty and our wells exhausted. Studying this Text still further we learn about people who "walked after vanity and became vain," [19] or, more truly translated, who "went after empty idols and became empty themselves," or, as it has also been rendered, who "following after the Bubble, bubbles became." This is precisely what happened to ourselves and our civilization. We followed bubbles, and we became bubbles, empty, iridescent, collapsible bubbles.

But admitting that this is a true description of our cultural history, how can we know whether there is meaning and unity and hope in the universe? Let us again study our Text, this time in the Book of Job. Job had suffered terribly. All his assumptions about life and God had been shattered. Whereupon the Almighty said to Job, "Where wast thou when I laid the foundations of the earth? When the morning stars sang together, and all the sons of God shouted for joy?" [20] By which He meant to say that, despite appearances and the jarring sounds of the present, the universe had been born to the strains of singing. The deeper music of history has not been the music of the anvil but the music of the harp, whose "tense strings" have accompanied a "new song," a sweet, redemptive melody. This song, whose theme is the "Word become flesh," the personal wisdom of God who became foolishness to redeem human folly, constitutes the deepest note in history, and proclaims the promise of a new order. Although it is often difficult to understand the music of life and history, the "new song" is always there, a strange harmony which only they can understand who are brought into sympathy of thought and life with the master Musician who is God Himself.

It is the function of Christian theology to interpret the original Text so that the strange music of life and its many jarring notes may be explained and that the music of God's new order may be learned. Theology cannot maintain itself in cloistered detachment from life, concerned solely with conceptions, no matter how true and pure these may be. It must come down from its balcony seat to where a confused multitude throngs the roadway and where ardent spirits join battle in the arena. Relating itself to the realities of life, theology must reinterpret to the milling crowd, to those locked in deadly strife, as well as to wayfarers and pilgrims on the

GOD AND CULTURE

march, the meaning of their existence and the hope of salvation. For what is really at stake at the present time in our cultural situation is the Christian conception of life. It is, therefore, the task of Christian theology so to study the confused human scene in the light of the Biblical text that meaning may be restored to life. When meaning is restored, and life is seen once more in the light of God and His purpose in Jesus Christ, great literature and great art, great philosophy and great politics, great preaching and great social change will come to us again.

But the restoration of meaning is not enough. *There must be also an experience of grace.* That significant and irreplaceable word "grace" has largely disappeared from American thought, both religious and secular. Grace means, in simplest terms, the good-will of God, and by an extension of meaning, the communication to life of His redemptive energy. For those who have experienced meaninglessness and perdition it is not enough that light should break, enabling them to understand themselves and their situation and to see the pathway to tomorrow. It is necessary that they experience renewal through the power symbolized by the sacred river that Ezekiel saw in vision, which, flowing forth from the sanctuary where the splendor of God had entered, turned Judean waste land into a garden, and the Dead Sea into a sea of life. Grace is that divine energy which makes every wilderness blossom and conquers death in all its forms.

Grace, as Augustine put it, is "the medicine of the soul working internally as drugs work externally upon the body." If our culture is to experience the reality of grace for its renewal, God must be admitted into life. Worship must become real. True worship, let us not forget, is worth-ship; it involves a sense of supreme value. It signifies the joyous self-dedication of life in all its spheres to God, the opening of its eastern gate and inmost recesses to His coming. Penitent confession of sin and failure, thankfulness to God for His great goodness, longing for inward purity, and the desire to become the channel of God's redemptive energy for the sake of others, are all part of true worship. But if worship means this, it follows that religion must be God-centred, and that the worshippers must be related directly to the living reality of God. A God-centred religion, however, is something totally different from a religion-centred God. Where religion, not God, is central, the unholy attempt is made to make Deity play a secondary role, accommodating Him to the schemes and caprices of the worshipper.

True worship is followed by work. Communion with the living God sends the worshipper back to living tasks. When men and women are earnest about life the spiritual refreshment derived from worship will not transform them into spectators of human affairs. It will rather clarify and deepen their sense of vocation. The artist who worships God in the "beauty of holiness," and is ravished by a glimpse of the Eternal Goodness, will discover a new sensitivity to form and acquire a creative sense of values. The scholar who, in the holy intimacy of worship, comes to know God who is "past finding out," will be inspired to make his knowledge available as a contribution to a Christian world-view. The business man will come forth from the worship of the "Father who worketh hitherto," eager to act in a way worthy of the chief Partner in his business. The statesman will leave the sanctuary where he has seen the "Lord high and lifted up," inspired

GOD AND CULTURE 79

to promote a political policy that shall reflect God's righteousness and mercy. The Christian college on whose staff are united different types of men and women of culture, bound together by a common faith, will prescribe to itself a double task. It will be the supreme glory of its teachers to meet with their students in the same creative intimacy in which God meets with them, and to work harmoniously together, each in his own sphere, in order to develop a full-orbed Christian conception of life.

Let me close with two passages from a statement drafted by a group of friends in two of Princeton's institutions of learning, and submitted by them to the second "Conference on Science, Philosophy and Religion." They will bring to a point the main thesis of this chapter: "In the Hebraic-Christian conception . . . the Divine is conceived in personal terms. Man's relationship with God is made possible by an antecedent act of revelation on His part. God reaches down to man in grace, man responds in gratitude and love. Moreover, since God is conceived primarily as moral will, and since His purpose is fulfilled in human life, man's task is not simply to contemplate ultimate reality and value, but to act in harmony with God's purpose for human life and history. Thus, intellectual and aesthetic contemplation is subordinated to practical moral action, and the values of both contemplation and action are so related to the all-embracing purposes of the Divine Spirit as to attain the deepest possible meaning."

"It is not primarily two different forms of govenment, but two different conceptions of human life, which are opposed in the life and death struggle of our day. Scholars must therefore do what it is so difficult for them to do in our 'liberal' culture: they must act as well as think. But they can act only if they will make up their minds on the great issues of the spiritual and moral life in which logical and scientific demonstration is impossible. They have a special responsibility, when fanatical loyalties rule one half of the world, to see that in the other half men reflect before they act. But they must also learn to commit themselves. For if commitment without reflection means fanaticism in action, reflection without commitment means a paralysis of all action. That way lies the death of democratic society and its culture." [21]

Reflection and commitment: First, the clarification and acceptance of truth about God; then the dedication of life to God and His purpose. Along that road lies the renovation of culture.

CHAPTER FIVE

GOD AND THE NATION

SOME TIME AGO a distinguished American made this statement: "Who can say that the prophet did not have America in his mind and the present day in his heart when he visioned the sun as a 'Sun of righteousness'? When he said in the last chapter of the Old Testament: 'For behold, the day that shall burn as an oven; and all the proud, yea, and all that do wickedly, shall be stubble: and the day that cometh shall burn them up, sayeth the Lord of Hosts, that it shall leave them neither root nor branch. But unto you that feareth my name shall the Sun of righteousness arise, with healing in its wings.'

"America, without pride of race but with complete tolerance and great power, can be that 'Sun of righteousness' with healing in its wings. America can establish the time of truly great peace based on justice to all the peoples." [1]

While such an interpretation of the prophet Malachi is very bad exegesis and still worse theology, the germinal concept of Vice-President Wallace that nations may be chosen by God for a providential role in history is perfectly sound and Biblical. Nations have sometimes fulfilled the divine purpose as the unconscious instruments of the will of God, as did Persia under Cyrus, and Greece and Rome in their time. Some nations in history have regarded themselves as called by God to be the executors of His will. Witness Spain in the sixteenth

82 HERITAGE AND DESTINY

century, invading the Low Countries and traversing the Western ocean as the "Arm of the Lord." Or consider Germany and Japan in the twentieth century, moved by what each regards as a cosmic mission. Sometimes the concern of nations has been to order their internal affairs in accordance with the divine will. This was the concern of Geneva in the time of John Calvin, the concern of England in the time of the Puritans, the concern of Scotland in the time of the Covenanters, and the concern of New England in the time of the Founding Fathers. Wherever this concern has been operative in the life of a people, the theocratic principle inherent in the life of Israel received contemporary expression. This chapter is a call to rethink the meaning of theocracy and a plea to recognize the abiding validity of the theocratic principle in the life of nations.

THEOCRACY, A QUESTION FOR TODAY

The theocratic idea which had inspired the national life of Israel at its best, and with which the Jewish sense of uniqueness and of destiny continues to be bound up, does not belong merely to history as a sociological conception now outmoded. It is as valid today, or, it might be said, more valid today, than at any previous period in world history since the dissolution of the nationhood of Israel. Although Israel ceased to be a nation in the first century of the Christian era, when the new Israel was born and Judea "was dissolved like a pearl in the cup of the universal communion," the covenant relation to God which had constituted the essence of Israel's nationhood has continued to be a pattern for the life of other national groups. In other words, Israel did not cease to have

GOD AND THE NATION 83

significance for history when it gave birth to the Christian Church, nor, since the Church was born, has the political significance of Israel been exhausted.

This contention is bound up, of course, with belief in the permanent validity of the Old Testament as a source of our knowledge of God's nature and will. So far from the Old Testament being out of date, and of exclusive interest as a repository of great thoughts upon religion, it has peculiar significance whenever a question arises regarding the relation between religion and politics, and the corporate responsibility of a people to God. No system of ethics can be fully Christian that leaves out of account the possibility of a nation's special relationship to God and the implications for conduct of such a relationship.

This is a problem which naturally did not interest, which, in fact, could not have interested, the New Testament writers, because of the special historical circumstances in which they lived. It is, however, a perennial problem upon which, paradoxically enough, the Old Testament has more guidance to give us than the New. Wherever and whenever Christians have found themselves in a situation where they were obliged to exercise political responsibility, the Old Testament, with its theocratic idea centering in the covenant between God and Israel, has taken on contemporary form. To put the matter simply, the heritage of Israel can be and should be the heritage of every nation, and the destiny of nations will be determined eventually by the seriousness or indifference with which they face and apply the covenant conception in their national life. It is the perennial human task "to make every land a Palestine," and the only international federation that can ultimately fulfill human destiny in the political realm will be a federation of theocratic states. The basis of true democracy is still, and will continue to be, theocracy.

TYPES OF NATIONHOOD

Let us begin this discussion by enquiring what is meant by the term "nation." Nation and nationhood may be defined from two different points of view. First: the secular principle of unity that binds together those who make up the "nation"; and second: the attitude which the nation takes up towards God and the divine.

Considered from *the viewpoint of a binding unity,* the meaning of nation has been admirably analyzed recently by a group of members of the Royal Institute of International Affairs. We cannot do better than follow their lucid and authoritative analysis. "Nation in English is used," these scholars say, "synonymously with 'State' or 'country' to mean a society united under one government. This sense of the term is not merely a usage of common speech, as the expressions 'Law of Nations,' 'League of Nations,' show. But the implications of 'nation' are never precisely those of 'State,' since 'nation' calls attention to those persons who compose a political community, 'State' to the sovereign power to which they owe an allegiance and which holds sway over the territory which they inhabit." A "nation," in this sense of the term, is frequently determined by frontiers of a physical or historical character. It is in this way, for example, that the Peruvian nation is constituted. Peruvian nationality is made up of diverse ethnical groups that have not yet been fused into a common culture. But the boundaries of the nation are determined by the frontier lines that date from the colonial period in South

GOD AND THE NATION 85

American history. Spain and Italy under the Fascist regime that rules them at present are also nations in this first sense.

Or nation may "denote an aggregation of individuals united by other, as well as political, ties—ties commonly of race, religion, language or tradition." These corporate individuals possess common institutions and common culture which give unity to the group and foster a spirit of sympathy between the members. In this usage "nation" is often contrasted with "state," while the connotation of the term is much richer and more vital than in the former instance. For here the bond that binds the so-called nation together is not geographical, historical, or even juridical in character, but is based primarily upon a common attitude towards life. It is thus that Russia, the Union of Soviet Republics, can be called a nation, despite the great variety of racial groups that make up the national unity. In this sense also the United States is a nation, despite the great diversity of background and type among its citizens. Great Britain and the members of the British Commonwealth of Nations are also nations in this supreme sense.

Nations, however, may be distinguished from each other in accordance with another principle: *the attitude which they take up towards God and the divine.*

There is, first, the *secular* nation. A secular nation is one which considers that public welfare demands the complete elimination of God from all official connection with its life and culture. It considers that its supreme loyalty is not to God but to ideas. Its heritage is not deity but ideology. It remains oblivious to the fact that the particular ideology to which it professes loyalty may be at bottom a kind of "secularized Christianity," an aspect of the national heritage

86 HERITAGE AND DESTINY

derived from a previous time when allegiance to God played a part in the life of the nation. The secular nation, however, does not interfere with freedom of thought or of religion on the part of individual citizens and private institutions in the country. Typical among secular nations are Uruguay and France. Early in the present century Uruguay set about eliminating every association with the Christian religion from all organizations and institutions controlled by the government. In the official calendar "Christmas Day" became "Family Day," and "Holy Week" was renamed "Touring Week."

The case of France is symbolic and ominous. Having lost all sense of the ultimate religious origin of the famous trio, "Liberty, Equality, Fraternity," which formed the slogan of the French Revolution, the rulers of the nation ceased to believe in the principles of democracy. All national sense of mission was lost. French political life became atomized into a multiplicity of groups. A sense of heritage disappeared, and with it a sense of destiny. When the nation suffered the onslaught of a people moved by a crusading sense of destiny there resulted one of the most amazing *débâcles* that ever marked the life of a great people.

The second type of nation is the *demonic* nation. The term "demonic" has been used in recent thought to connote the absolutization of the relative, that is to say, the elevation into an absolute of something purely relative and finite. A demonic nation is one which has transformed itself into an ultimate, taking the place of God, or has deified some reality associated with its life. The four totalitarian nations in the world of today are all demonic in character. The demonic element in each case is identical with that reality which the

GOD AND THE NATION

nation regards as its true heritage. In Chapter One we had occasion to consider how each totalitarian nation reached its sense of heritage by a retrospective process. We shall consider the most typical demonic nation of our time with particular reference to its religious significance.

The outstanding example of a demonic nation is Germany. Following a psychological process which becomes operative in times of crisis, and which has already been analyzed, the German *volk* became elevated into the virtual status of deity.

At a psychologically propitious moment the totalitarian state idea derived from Hegel, and the deified people idea derived from Fichte and Houston Chamberlain, became personalized in a messianic figure, the Fuehrer, God manifest in the flesh, who took the place of Jesus Christ. The Fuehrer created a new state in which the German people was invited to do obeisance at its own shrine. The result was a florid, mystical paganism. The record of the Fuehrer's life and thought—"Mein Kampf"—became the new Bible of the holy German nation. The fellowship of a political party took the place of the Christian Church. At party meetings a gorgeous pagan ritual played the part of the traditional Christian liturgy. The myth of the twentieth century usurped the role of Christian Theology. Missionaries began to invade every land to prepare for the coming of the new messiah and to make his way easy when the "day" should come. Missionary fifth columnists, and soldiers who today fight with the primitive fury of dervishes, have all been inspired by the messianic vision of a new age. Some day the glory of the German people would "cover the earth as the waters cover the channels of the deep." Then the world would acknowledge its true master and its life would be organized upon the pattern of a new order. In this way a great people assumed the attributes and role of deity, covenanting to give the world no respite and itself no repose until its racial destiny should be fulfilled on a world scale.

The *covenant* nation is the third type of nation. Such a nation is one which recognizes its dependence upon God and its responsibility towards God. The covenant idea has sometimes been expressed by a state church as in England, Scotland, and Norway. A state church is a symbol that the nation which supports it recognizes an allegiance higher than the state and state interests. It is sadly true, of course, that so-called state churches have many a time been no more than creatures of government. Not infrequently, however, a state church has dared to confront and denounce government in the name of God. We think instinctively of the Scottish Church in the times of John Knox and of Thomas Chalmers and of the glorious Norwegian Church in these days of Hitler and Quisling.

In still other cases the covenant idea has been expressed in the constitution and national institutions of a country. In the case in the United States of America, God is acknowledged as the source of human rights in the immortal Declaration of Independence, while the words "In God We Trust" are engraven on the humblest coin in the national currency. A study of the Declaration of Independence makes it clear that, in the judgment of the framers, it is not to reason or to revolution that we owe our liberty, but to the fact that God made man. It is all too true, alas, that in many highways and byways of the political, as well as the social, life of the American people, cynics may find ground for asking what God it is in whom trust is thus reposed. Is the

GOD AND THE NATION

American God wealth, or comfort, or a standard of living, or rugged individualism? These questions are pertinent, but the fact remains that this nation, in the beginning of its history when it was still a colony of England, covenanted with God in a very unique sense, and that later, when the Republic was born, God was recognized as the source of human rights.

THIS COVENANT NATION

When we speak of the United States as an example of a covenant nation, we are very far from thinking of it as a perfect model of nationhood, or as a nation that is the favorite of Deity. For God has no favorites in our human sense. Nor is our national righteousness, to use the Biblical phrase, any more than "filthy rags" in the presence of God's moral purity and the majesty of our moral responsibility. A covenant nation is simply one which, whatever its shortcomings, recognizes that God and His purposes stand above the nation and the nation's interests, and that the highest role a nation can play is to reflect God's righteousness in national policy and promote His purposes in all life's relationships. When we plead, therefore, that the American people face squarely their special relationship to God and their special responsibility towards God, we would not be accused of Americanizing God or of trying to arouse faith in a national deity who had chosen the people of this republic to be His chosen folk. If we meant that, we should be advocating a religious attitude identical with that of the Germans and Japanese who have made religion the power-house of politics. No; what we plead for rather is that we examine ourselves, our past, present, and future, in the searching light of God.

The subject of American destiny has become distasteful to a multitude of our best citizens because of the repugnance aroused by the "hundred percent Americans" and the braggadocio of the "manifest destiny" school. And there has been good reason for this. That prince of American journalists, the late John H. Finley, of the *New York Times,* tells of a famous toast once given in Paris by a certain American of this reprehensible type, "I give you the United States," said this paragon of modesty, "bounded on the north by the Aurora Borealis, on the south by the procession of the equinoxes, on the east by primeval chaos, and on the west by the Day of Judgment." [2]

It is the spirit symbolized by this toast that has made a certain type of Americanism objectionable to the world at large, as well as to the best citizens of their own country. Yet the obligation to face the question of American destiny is quite inescapable. So, ridding our minds of every arrogant suggestion regarding a "chosen" people, and rejecting both the exegesis and the theology that would make this country the Biblical "Sun of righteousness," even though they have presidential sanction, let us ask, Whither are we bound? Whither should we be bound? These questions can be answered only after we have asked ourselves this other, Whence have we come? Who and what are we? We cannot speak with any truth or realism about tomorrow until we have looked back into the face of yesterday.

But how it irks people to look back who have been so long accustomed to look forward! Having identified progress so exclusively with the forward look and with movement and speed, it is difficult for Americans to believe that yesterday has important lessons for today. The latest object or idea has

GOD AND THE NATION

always seemed to us the best. And when we do look back it is with the childish eyes of sentimentalists who merely glorify the by-gone. For we love historical associations, and relics, and souvenirs, more than any people. Or else we become interested in the past because we want our prejudices to be confirmed—that isolationism, for example, is the true American doctrine. But we fail to study our history in order to acquire a sense of tradition, or to come to know and possess our heritage, or to discover landmarks in the realm of yesterday that can guide us on through today into tomorrow. And yet the most creative and steadying word in human speech is the word "remember."

It is important that we consider with reverence and awe what we are and the heritage into which we have entered. If the ancient Israelites were accustomed to contrast their country with Egypt out of which they came, speaking of it as a "land of hills and valleys that drank water of the rain of heaven," we in this country have reason to thank God with awe for a unique physical inheritance. From the Atlantic to the Pacific the country is replete with parables of exuberant nature. The giant redwoods of California were young when Abraham left Ur of the Chaldees along the road of destiny. These are symbols of biological riches. The oil derricks that rear their heads in so many states of the union, from Pennsylvania, where oil wells were first drilled, to the Pacific Coast, are emblems of mineral wealth.

But this is nothing compared with our human heritage. In no country in history have the inhabitants constituted such a vast racial microcosm of mankind. It is no wonder that we do not possess a national instrument of music. Greece had its pipe and its lyre, Rome its trumpet, Germany its cathedral organ, Ireland its harp, and Scotland its bagpipes. But the music of America must ever be the orchestra in which all national and racial instruments are blended. In this orchestra the deep bass notes are produced by our great Negro population, which has contributed more than any other racial group to American minstrelsy. With such a heritage our destiny can never be fulfilled until inter-racial relations in this country take on a rich orchestral harmony.

It is sometimes said, with a great deal of truth, that America has neither history nor historical sense. Paradoxically enough, this fact constitutes a most important part of our heritage. Our very lack of history has saved us from the dread "pathology of the frontier," which has been one of the chief sources of European wars. For happily there does not exist anywhere near our borders a Rhine or a Polish Corridor, nor any frontier the mere mention of which awakens the sentiment of hatred or revenge. In Europe, "frontier" has signified "a fortified boundary between densely populated regions"; in this country it has meant traditionally "the hither side of free land."

Here is another historical paradox. How strange that a country which, compared with Europe, Asia, and Africa, has no history, should be nevertheless an epitome of all history! This fact was strikingly pointed out by Frederick Jackson Turner, that great student of American frontier development. In the words of this historian: "We have a recurrence of the process of evolution in each western area reached in the process of expansion. Thus American development has exhibited not merely advance along a single line, but a return to primitive conditions on a continually advanc-

GOD AND THE NATION 93

ing frontier line, and a new development for that area. American social development has been continually beginning over again on the frontier. This perennial rebirth, this fluidity of American life, this expansion westward with its new opportunities, its continuous touch with the simplicity of primitive society, furnish the forces dominating American character." [3] He then goes on to quote Loria, the Italian economist, who had urged the study of colonial life as an aid to understanding the stages of European development. "America," says Loria, "has the key to the historical enigma which Europe has sought for centuries in vain, and the land which has no history reveals luminously the course of universal history." [4] But surely, if it is part of our human heritage that American history, such as it is, has epitomized the development of mankind, and still continues, in different areas of the country, to epitomize the varying conditions in which mankind finds itself today, this fact constitutes an imperious call to us. It summons every American to think in terms of mankind as a whole, and to share with others on a world scale our experience and resources.

Our Spiritual Heritage

But greatest and most significant of all has been our spiritual heritage, our religious tradition. The core of this tradition is a spiritual reality, the reality of God. God in the most concrete sense was the heritage of the Founding Fathers of the nation. The American people covenanted with God, not as a local, continental, or racial deity, but as the living, universal God who, while being the God of all people, becomes in a very special sense the God of all those who accept His purpose for human life. Apart from faith in God

American history has no meaning. In this faith our institutions were created, our laws enacted, and our liberties secured. By the light of this faith culture was promoted, its warmth enkindled philanthropic and missionary endeavor throughout the world. Christian missionaries were the first American internationalists and this country's greatest ambassadors of goodwill to all parts of the globe.

Far be it from me to suggest that we become traditionalists and bind ourselves to a changeless yesterday. I merely state a fact which we dare not ignore, least of all in a time of crisis. The fact is this. This country was founded in religious faith. Whether we think of the English Puritans or the Irish and Scotch, the Germans, Dutch, and Scandinavians, and many other groups who moved westward from the Atlantic seaboard and fanned out across the continent, faith in God was common to them all. Differences there were among them, Quakers and Presbyterians, Anglicans, Methodists, and Baptists, Catholics of French, Spanish and Irish stock. All, however, were committed to an interpretation of life which made human welfare in its individual and corporate aspects dependent upon the service of a God who was not the patrimony of their several racial traditions, whose interests were not confined to the Western world and its people, but who was the God of the whole earth, revealed supremely in the history of Israel and in personal terms in Jesus Christ.

Inasmuch, however, as the influence of religion in the colonization and development of the United States has been disputed, or very much ignored in recent times, it becomes necessary to validate our contention with some concrete and detailed references. Such a task has been made easier in the

GOD AND THE NATION

last few years because of the admirable work of a group of Harvard historians. These distinguished men, while not sharing the religious ideas of the Puritans who founded New England, have felt called upon to vindicate their memory and to show the creative part that Puritan religion played in the development of American history and institutions. No one can deny, nor is it necessary to deny, that the economic motive and the love of adventure played their own part in the settling of New England. But the dynamic force was religious in character. Says one of these Harvard historians: "No one who has delved deeply into the origin and history of the New England colonies can, by any fair application of the rules of evidence, deny that the dynamic force in settling New England was English Puritanism desiring to realize itself. The leaders, whom the people followed, proposed like Milton to make over a portion of the earth in the spirit of Christian philosophy: a new church and state, family and school, ethic and conduct. They might and did differ among themselves as to the realization of these high and holy aims, but a new City of God was their aim. . . . Religion should permeate every phase of living. Man belongs to God alone: his only purpose in life was to enhance God's glory and do God's will; and every variety of human activity, every sort of human conduct, presumably unpleasing to God, must be discouraged if not suppressed."[5]

Another of these distinguished historians[6] has analyzed the New England mind, and finds that the religious thought and attitudes of the early settlers in New England were dominated by a sense of three great realities: God, sin, and regeneration. In an age in which the sermon was the outstanding product of literary activity, the Puritans lived in the daily and hourly presence of a majestic, almighty God. They had a realistic outlook upon sinful human nature, knowing "what was in man." But the possibility and reality of regenerative change filled them with a sublime optimism, for the power of God was equal to every human situation. Despite the grim fact of sin and its baleful consequences, renewal was gloriously possible through the redeeming love and power of the Almighty.

The characteristic attitudes and ideas of representative Puritans received personalized expression in the life history of a family, the Mathers. Murdock, in his life of Increase Mather, makes special reference to Richard Mather, the father of Increase and his brother Cotton. The spiritual experience through which Richard Mather passed when a young man in Lancashire, England, is a parable of the New England attitude and outlook in the early period. "Some time in 1614," says Murdock, "there sat beneath a hedge in Lancashire a boy of eighteen, weeping bitterly 'to lament his misery before God.' Such was Richard Mather's religious coming of age. Boy as he was, the effect of Puritan teaching was for him an intense conviction of the power of the Lord, and of his own unworthiness. His emotion drove him from the hospitable table of Edward Aspinwall, of Troxteth, near Liverpool, to seek solitude for repentance and prayer. From this dawning of religious feeling sprang his consecration to the Puritan Church. With his boyish fears at his first spiritual awakening, began his unswerving devotion to his faith, passed on as a heritage to his descendents, and transformed by him and them into service which brought renown to their family name."[7]

The passionate devotion to God exemplified on this

GOD AND THE NATION 97

continent by the New England Puritans and subsequently expressed in the life of the new nation by other religious groups from the continent of Europe, became the fountainhead of culture, of freedom, of enterprise, of social responsibility, and of missionary zeal. The religious origin of the American concern for culture, to take but one typical instance, is classically expressed in the inscription carved on the college gate at Harvard: "After God had carried us safe to New England and we had builded our houses, provided necessaries for our livelihood, reared convenient places for God's worship, and settled the civil government, one of the next things we longed for and looked after was to advance learning and perpetuate it to posterity, ready to leave a literate ministry to the churches when our present ministers shall lie in the dust." One can count upon the fingers of one hand the institutions of higher learning in this country, of front line calibre, of a private character, and interested in the humanities, which have not had a religious origin. Let us call the roll. Harvard and Yale were founded by Congregationalists; the Universities of Columbia and of Pennsylvania by Episcopalians; Princeton by Presbyterians; Duke and Northwestern by Methodists; the University of Chicago by Baptists; Fordham and Notre Dame by Roman Catholics; while the great University of California, now a state institution, was founded by two clergymen, one a Congregationalist and the other a Presbyterian.

It was also among religious groups that the spirit of democratic freedom was fostered. The name of Roger Williams will be forever associated with the foundations of religious liberty in this country. Men accustomed to freedom in their personal approach to God insisted upon freedom in the public expression of their ideas and the ordering of their lives. Nine graduates of the little College of New Jersey, of which John Witherspoon was President, were among the drafters of the national Constitution. Under the influence of Witherspoon, who first in Scotland and later in America, had been a champion of liberty and was the only clergyman to sign the Declaration of Independence, the state of New Jersey led the colonies with a Constitution that granted the most absolute religious freedom.

The spirit of the Protestant Reformation, mediated to the life of America by the English Puritans and by other Protestant groups that came to this country in the eighteenth and nineteenth centuries, promoted a sense of religious vocation in civic and business life. All work was counted honorable and was entered into with zest. Private initiative was encouraged and carried through. In the course of time, when the products of toil accumulated, they were, in numberless instances, not hoarded or selfishly used, but, to an extent unparalleled in history, were devoted to great causes, civic, cultural, philanthropic, and missionary. Nothing in the life of North America has so impressed reflective minds in the Southern continent as the extent to which many great fortunes have been used, not for selfish ends, but for human welfare in one phase or another.

THE HERITAGES OF DON QUIXOTE AND ROBINSON CRUSOE

The mention of the lands to the south of us, where some of the happiest years of my life were spent, suggests a comparison between two types of civilization, that of Anglo-Saxon America and that of Hispanic America. This comparison will help to define still more clearly the specific

GOD AND THE NATION

heritage of the United States as a covenant nation. We shall select for the purpose the contrasted figures of two profoundly symbolical men.

The character and history of two famous personages of fiction, one a Spaniard, the other an Englishman, are perfect parables of the civilizations to which each belonged. Don Quixote, the Spanish knight, and Robinson Crusoe, the shipwrecked English sailor, are the prototypes respectively of the two Americas, the America that bears the indelible impress of Hispania, the old name for Spain and Portugal, and the other that bears the indelible stamp of England. There are three main points of comparison between the two men, centering in the origin, the aim, and the inspiration of their great adventures.

One bright July morning, fully armed and mounted upon his steed, Don Quixote sallied forth to the song of birds to change the world. Perfect picture of the favorable circumstances in which the Spanish empire was born. In the spring of 1492, after seven centuries of deadly strife between Cross and Crescent, the banners of Castile and Aragon waved from the turrets of the Moorish Alhambra. In the fall of the same year a Genoese mariner, Christopher Columbus, announced the discovery of the Indies. Spain accepted a new world as God's gift for her loyalty, and embarked upon its conquest in His name.

Robinson Crusoe was hurled upon an inhospitable shore from a wrecked ship, borne upon the crests of ocean billows. So came the Pilgrims to "this American wilderness." Leaving England in a political tempest, they weathered storms on the Western ocean, and settled at last in the least suitable part of the Atlantic seaboard. They thought nothing of empire, but only of freedom to live their lives in accordance with the will of God.

The aim of Quixote was to impose upon human relations his own knightly but abstract sense of justice, righting wrongs wherever he went. The regimentation of the lives and relations of others became the keynote of Spanish colonial policy, which reached its most classical expression in the Jesuit Empire in Paraguay. Spaniards did not work but made others work. A premium was thus put upon professionalism, producing an attitude towards manual labor which has continued to this day, while the state as the creation and instrument of the traditional professional classes, came to be regarded as the purveyor of all good things.

Robinson Crusoe was obliged to work or perish. He accordingly set himself to labor and transformed his island home into a garden. So worked the Puritans in arid New England hills, where they built their homesteads and reared and educated their families. True to the Reformed tradition in which they had been reared, all work was considered honorable and a part of God's plan for each life. The result was disciplined lives, free enterprise, and unprecedented productivity.

The chief difference, however, between the two civilizations is symbolized in the contrasted sources of inspiration that made the Spanish knight an administrator of justice and the English sailor a disciplined apostle of work. Quixote's brain was fired, not to say turned, by reading a whole library of books on knight errantry. These were the precursors of the innumerable volumes of idealism in which Hispanic Americans have revelled. Children of Erasmus rather than of Luther, they are more widely read than any similar group in the world. Their great newspapers have finer news services than those of North America; and their splendid "book palaces" stock a greater variety of literature than typical American book stores do. The constitutions of Hispano-American countries are epitomes of the most ideal elements in the great constitutions of the world, even though, in certain cases, they may prove inapplicable to the conditions prevailing in the lands they are designed to rule.

In an old sea chest where he was searching for tobacco to cure a tropical fever, Crusoe found a Bible. As a result of reading it, he passed through a deep evangelical conversion, as significant and far-reaching as that of Richard Mather. "Jesus, thou exalted Prince and Savior! give me repentance!" were the words of his anguished prayer. The Book opened up to him a strange new world which transformed his life. The Bible, which has been traditionally unknown by the classes and the masses in the Hispanic world, has been the supreme spiritual influence in North American civilization. It has produced a spiritual inwardness which, according to the heads of two Argentine Universities, Ricardo Rojas and Juan B. Terán, and that greatest of Spanish men of letters, Miguel de Unamuno, has been entirely lacking in the religious life of Hispanic American lands.

What is best in North American life, the precious ore amid much dross, we owe to the heritage that came to us, not from books in general, but from a Book, and from the spiritual awakenings produced by the Book upon innumerable spiritual children of Robinson Crusoe and Richard Mather. According to distinguished South American writers Hispanic America is a wilderness so far as knowledge of the Bible is concerned. In their view, the greatest single need of culture, of politics, and of religion in those great southern lands is a first-hand knowledge of the Book of books. Talk about inter-American cultural relations will be vain and unproductive, North and South America will never understand each other fully, their destinies will never truly merge, until both rediscover, and express in life, the Hebrew-Christian heritage with which the destiny of the Western world and of the world as a whole is bound up.

THE FULFILLMENT OF NATIONAL DESTINY

After this rather lengthy excursion into national history and continental civilization, we return once again to the question, Whither are we bound as a nation? The destiny of this country is inseparably bound up with loyalty to its national heritage. As already stated, apart from faith in God the history of America has no meaning. The greatest spiritual task that confronts us consists in interpreting for our time the meaning of the motto inscribed on each copper penny, "In God We Trust," and in applying that interpretation to our national and international policy.

History teaches us that nations often miss their way and fail to fulfill their destiny. The tragedy of Israel has constantly been repeated along the road of the ages. When this has happened it has not been due to any cosmic, logic, or irrational chance, or the failure to ride some "wave of the future." It has been due, and will always be due, to the failure to abide by the principles of that practical wisdom which derives from the fear of God. *Initium Sapientiae Timor*

GOD AND THE NATION 103

Domini is the motto of a great University, dear to the writer.[8] Apart from *timor Domini,* or in St. Augustine's phrase, *adhaerere Deo,* there can be no purity, stability, or permanence in the life of a nation.

But if the reality of *timor Domini* is regnant in the life of a nation, there is no reason in the nature of things why that nation should suffer dissolution and cease to be a power, whether political or spiritual, in God's world. Cochrane, in his great book, "Christianity and Classical Culture," quotes the words in which the Emperor Augustus expressed the grounds of his hope to an abiding place in history: "May it be my privilege to establish the republic safe and sound on its foundations, gathering the fruit of my desire to be known as author of the ideal constitution, and taking with me to the grave the hope that the basis which I have laid will be permanent."[9] Augustus dreamed of the eternity of Rome, but a man called Gibbon lived to write "The Decline and Fall of the Roman Empire." Today another man, called Mussolini, dreams, if he is still capable of dreaming, of restoring the empire of Augustus. The fall of Rome was inevitable because the Empire, despite Constantine, was not founded upon political principles which derived from *timor Domini,* nor was ruled by men who were inspired by the loyalty enshrined in *adhaerere Deo*. But it is not necessary that a nation which has access to the full light of the Christian revelation for its political direction, and which is seriously convinced that a nation primarily exists to serve God, should pass irrevocably away. It is not inevitable, therefore, that the American nation, if loyal to its heritage, should suffer decay. There is power in the God who comes to us in the Hebrew-Christian tradition, which is our heritage, to pilot us through the darkness and neutralize all the natural tendencies to impotence and dissolution.

But if we are to fulfill our destiny in God's world and not perish from the earth, very costly commitments devolve upon us.

First: The American Caesar must take pains to acknowledge and express the lordship of God. In doing so, the nation must face afresh the Man of destiny in whom God expressed His will for mankind, and who is today the Sovereign Lord. Although Jesus Christ said that His kingdom was not *of* this world, He did not mean that it had nothing to do *with* this world. His Kingdom has to do in a very real sense with the affairs of men, from the private conduct of all citizens to the public policies of the men in authority. Caesar today can find his role and fulfill it, in the providential rule of God, only by realizing that constructive political action must be inspired in the supreme values and purposes that belong to the Kingdom of Christ. Only at his peril will Caesar run counter in his schemes and attitudes to that allegiance which persons and peoples owe to God.

Second: Penitence is called for. Although the orchestra is the only adequate expression of American music, relations between racial groups in this country have not produced the orchestral melody which they ought. Deep penitence becomes us also because, if the Germans and Japanese, with whom we fight today, are what they are, we must share a large part of the responsibility for having made them what we now find them to be. Our attitude towards them was the repudiation of faith in God and of responsibility to man.

GOD AND THE NATION

Third: God, our supreme heritage, who loves all men and works for the coming of a world community, commits this nation to recognize the inherent rights of all individuals and peoples to a free and equal opportunity to choose their own way and express their own life within the limits imposed by the rights of others. This would involve commitment to seek a world federation of equal peoples, and to purge American life from everything in class and race relations that denies the reality of human brotherhood.

Fourth: In this time of deep crisis, when nations which we have called "demonic" have deliberately rejected subjection to God and to any authority outside their own national and racial selves, and seek by force to impose an order from which the great freedoms would be excluded, the covenant nation becomes inexorably arrayed against them in the sphere of political reality. The United States is, therefore, committed as a nation to accept the responsibility which God, in His providential economy, lays upon states such as ours to provide a political order in which principles of righteousness may receive concrete social expression. It becomes the responsibility of the American state, in a world in which the most elemental principles of human right are denied, to employ force for the restraint of evil and the establishment of an order of justice. This nation has the inescapable obligation to wage the present war to a finish, not as a holy war or as a Christian cause—for no war can be holy, and no political cause can be fully Christian—but as a necessary, though disagreeable, police measure. And this it must do, gambling its existence and destiny upon the fulfillment throughout the world of its own early vision of human freedom under God.

Thus God, the ancient heritage of Israel, the transforming patrimony of the soul, and the everlasting well-spring of culture, must become the chosen heritage of this and every nation of mankind, if human destiny is to be worthily fulfilled within the framework of world order tomorrow.

NOTES

CHAPTER ONE

[1] *El Hombre como Método*, Humberto Palza S., San Francisco de California, 1939.
[2] Psalm 73:25, 26.
[3] Psalm 16:2, 4, 5, 6, 11.
[4] *Vid. Mussolini's Italy*, Herman Finer, Henry Holt & Co., p. 19.

CHAPTER TWO

[1] *God in History*, James Strahan, James Clarke & Co., Ltd., London, p. 15.
[2] The study of the Old Testament has suffered greatly from the use of alien categories. "May it not be regarded as a major disaster in the history of Biblical studies," says a very able English writer, that "Biblical students should have been busily engaged in interpreting the Bible by categories alien to itself. They have been treating it in evolutionary terms as the story of a development of Israel. But Israel herself thought of her story as one of a call and a vocation." (*The Throne of David*, A. G. Hebert, p. 29).
[3] Deuteronomy 4:20.
[4] Deuteronomy 32:9.
[5] Jeremiah 51:19.
[6] Psalms 73:26.
[7] Psalms 119:57.
[8] *The Chief End of Revelation*, Alexander Balmain Bruce, Hodder and Stoughton, London, p. 116.
[9] *Man in Revolt*, Emil Brunner, R. T. S., Lutterworth Press, London, p. 448.
[10] Hosea 4:6.
[11] Hosea 7:11.
[12] Isaiah 51:1-2.
[13] Ezekiel 43:4.
[14] Ezekiel 47:1.
[15] Zechariah 14:8-9.
[16] *Paul Among the Jews*, Franz Werfel, A. R. Mowbray & Co., Ltd.
[17] *Id.*, pp. 138-140, 144, 150.
[18] *Id.*, p. 145.

[19] Quoted in *God in History*, James Strahan, James Clarke & Co., Ltd., London, p. 178.
[20] *Atlantic Monthly*, December 1937.

CHAPTER THREE

[1] *Christianity and Civilization*, Arnold J. Toynbee, pp. 22, 48.
[2] *Ibid.*, pp. 38–40.
[3] Job 15:14.
[4] *Id.*, 25:4.
[5] *Man In Revolt*, Emil Brunner, R. T. S., Lutterworth Press, London, p. 494.
[6] *Id.*, p. 52.
[7] Luke 15:19.
[8] *The Puritan Pronaos*, Samuel Eliot Morison, pp. 9–11.
[9] *Rembrandt*, G. Baldwin Brown, p. 108.
[10] *J. S. Bach*, Albert Schweitzer, p. 306.
[11] *Edward Wilson of the Antarctic*, George Seaver, John Murray, pp. 293–294.
[12] *Id.*, p xxxii.

CHAPTER FOUR

[1] *Spiritual Aspects of the New Poetry*, Amos N. Wilder, Harper & Brothers, p. 100.
[2] Quoted by Wilder in *Spiritual Aspects of the New Poetry*, p. 101.
[3] *Ibid.*, p. 101.
[4] Quoted in *The American Scholar* from "Banality on the March" by Peter Viereck, July 1941.
[5] Quoted by Wilder in *Spiritual Aspects of the New Poetry*, p. 10.
[6] T. S. Stribling in *These Bars of Flesh*.
[7] T. S. Eliot in *The Wasteland*.
[8] Quoted in *The American Scholar* for July 1941.
[9] Isaiah 50:11 (E. R. V.).
[10] Quoted in Henry C. Link's *The Rediscovery of Man*, The Macmillan Company, p. 88.
[11] Cf. Monier, *Personalist Manifesto*.
[12] *Science, Philosophy and Religion* (first symposium), pp. 123–138.
[13] Quoted in *Spiritual Aspects of the New Poetry*, by Wilder, p. 193.
[14] St. John 1:14.
[15] Psalm 36:9.
[16] *J. S. Bach*, Albert Schweitzer, The Macmillan Company, Vol. I, p. VI.
[17] Isaiah 2:22.
[18] Jeremiah 2:13.

[19] *Id.*, 2:5.
[20] Job 38:4, 7.
[21] *Science, Philosophy and Religion* (second symposium), Conference on Science, Philosophy, and Religion in Their Relation to the Democratic way of Life, Inc., pp. 254, 256. The Princeton statement was signed by J. Douglas Brown, Theodore M. Greene, E. H. Harbison, Whitney J. Oates, Henry Norris Russell, Hugh S. Taylor, George F. Thomas, John A. Mackay.

CHAPTER FIVE

[1] *Why Did God Make America?* Address by Hon. Henry A. Wallace, United States Government Printing Office.
[2] *The Coming of the Scot,* John H. Finley, Charles Scribner's Sons, p. 98.
[3] *The Frontier in American History,* Frederick Jackson Turner, Henry Holt and Company, pp. 2–3.
[4] *Id.*, p. 11.
[5] *The Puritan Pronaos,* Samuel Eliot Morison, New York University Press, pp. 6–7.
[6] Perry Miller, in *The New England Mind*.
[7] *Increase Mather,* Kenneth Ballard Murdock, Harvard University Press, p. 11.
[8] The University of Aberdeen.
[9] *Christianity and Classical Culture,* Charles Norris Cochrane, Clarendon Press, p. 1.

www.ingramcontent.com/pod-product-compliance
Lightning Source LLC
Chambersburg PA
CBHW071220160426
43196CB00012B/2358